THE CALL I ALMOST MISSED

The Call I Almost Missed

365 Days Without a Cell Phone
and What It Taught Me About Love,
Presence, and the Lies We Live

Tommy Short

THE CALL I ALMOST MISSED
*365 Days Without a Cell Phone and What It Taught
Me About Love, Presence, and the Lies We Live*

FIRST EDITION

ISBN   978-1-5445-5150-0   *Hardcover*
       978-1-5445-5149-4   *Paperback*
       978-1-5445-5148-7   *Ebook*

For my girls, Giuliana and Natalia:

You were never asking for perfection. Only presence.

This book is my yes.

Contents

Foreword

—DERICK GRANT, MINDSET COACH

Life is simple. Complicated at times, sure, but still simple. Along this journey we call life, we ride the ups and downs, measuring so much of it by how we feel. The highs affirm what the lows came to teach us. But most people, unfortunately, don't use the downs for what they were designed to do: help us grow. Every now and then, though, you meet someone who's *different*.

Different because they took their hardest, most painful moments and turned them into fuel. *Different* because they didn't quit when life hit back. *Different* because they understood something most people don't—that the journey itself is more rewarding than any destination. *Different* because they've learned how to walk into the depths of their own soul, gather the lost, fractured pieces of who they used to be, and turn them into wisdom.

Tommy Short is one of those different people.

As a mindset coach, I've had the privilege of working with some of the best athletes, entrepreneurs, and leaders in the world. The common thread among all the great ones isn't just talent, it's the willingness to walk straight into discomfort, knowing that growth is waiting on the other side of pain. That's what I've seen in Tommy.

I met him about four years ago, and since then, I've had a front-row seat to his transformation. I've seen his strength, his courage, and his faith, especially when life didn't go the way he planned. When he told me he was giving up his cell phone for an entire year, I thought he was joking. But then it hit me, *this* is what makes him different. Most people look for ways to escape their storms. Tommy walks into them. He understands that sometimes the rain has to fall to wash away what we can't remove ourselves. I've watched him stand face-to-face with things that would have broken most people.

Losing his mother, facing profound challenges in his closest relationships, questioning who he was and where he was going, and yet every single time, he stayed with it. He didn't run from the pain. He let it refine him. That kind of courage can't be taught. It comes from a soul that has already decided, "No matter what, I'm going to grow from this." Tommy's story isn't just about struggle; it's about surrender. He's learned that healing doesn't come from fixing what's wrong, but from remembering who you've always been. He's turned pain into purpose, heartbreak into humility, and fear into faith. And through it all, he's done it with a grace that only comes from someone who's walked through fire and came out glowing.

This book is a reflection of that journey. It's a guide, an invitation, and a mirror. Inside these pages, you'll find pieces of your own story. You'll see yourself in the questions, the breakthroughs, and the moments of surrender. Because what Tommy has done isn't just for him. It's a roadmap for anyone ready to stop running from life and start walking with it. If you let this book in, it won't just change how you think. It'll change how you see. You'll start to notice that even the hardest moments were never meant to destroy you; they were meant to awaken you. You'll realize that the storms weren't punishment, they were preparation.

Tommy Short is living proof that when you stop resisting life, you start receiving it. His journey reminds us that it's not about what happens to you, but what you choose to become because of it. So take a breath. Open your heart. And allow these words to meet you exactly where you are. In reality, the truth is, life has always been happening for you. Once you finally see that, you'll become different too.

FAQs

1. Did you really go an entire year without a phone? Like, none at all?

Yes. No iPhone. No flip phone. No landline. No burner. No emergency workaround. If you needed me, you had to find me in person or through email—or wait.

2. Why would you do that? Was this a tech detox? A stunt? A midlife crisis?

Fair question. On paper, it makes no sense. I'm a speaker by trade; words are my work. Logistics are my life. I've lived most of my adult years wired to be reachable. But then my daughter asked me why I was on my phone all the time. I had to admit to myself that she was right, and I couldn't ignore that. Something cracked open in me.

3. How old are you? Where do you live? Were you off-grid in a cabin somewhere?

I'm in my forties. I live in the suburbs. Two daughters. A business. A mortgage. I didn't disappear into the woods. I just got quiet in the middle of regular life.

4. What about emergencies? Or work? Or your family needing you?

Those questions haunted me, too. But what I found was that most of what we call "emergencies" aren't. And the people who really needed me? They found me. Or they learned to trust I'd be there, just not instantly.

5. Was your wife on board? Did your family support this?

Not exactly. It created tension—some of it tender, some of it sharp. You'll see that unfold in the pages to come. This journey didn't just challenge me. It also changed me. It stretched everyone around me, too.

6. How did your wife get in touch with you?

It's a good question—and the first question many women ask me when they hear about my project. The answer is mainly through email. We both worked from home, so our situation wasn't as complicated as it could be for other couples.

7. Did you announce it? Or just vanish?

I told the people who needed to know. But there was no grand gesture. No social media goodbye post. I wasn't trying to be impressive. I was trying to be honest. With myself first.

8. What surprised you the most?

That many things don't matter as much as we think they do, and can wait. And that presence isn't about proximity; it's about attention. And that growth doesn't always feel like blooming. Sometimes, it feels like unraveling.

9. Did you miss anything? Would you do it again?

I missed convenience. I missed control. But I didn't miss my life—I found it. And yes, I'd do it again. But this time, I'd start sooner.

10. Why write this book? Why in the form of letters to your daughters?

Because I've spent a lot of my life using words—to speak, to inspire, to lead others. But this year taught me that the most important words aren't the ones said in board rooms. They're said in bedrooms and kitchens and in the car while driving your children to school. They're the ones written in margins, spoken when no one's watching. These letters are for my daughters—but maybe, if you've ever felt lost or numb or ready for something deeper, they're for you, too.

What is the question that changed everything?

(DAY 1)

Dear Girls,

It was a Saturday that smelled like summer, the kind of day where time feels soft around the edges. No alarm clocks, no chaos getting ready for school, just cereal bowls, sunlight on the floor, and a living room full of plastic princess shoes and belly laughs.

I was on the couch. You two were dancing in pajamas with wild hair and wild hearts.

And then, without any ceremony or warning, Giuliana, you turned to me and asked a question that would change everything:

"Daddy, why are you always on your phone?"

You weren't angry. You were confused. You were noticing. You saw something I hadn't yet dared to see in myself. And that question stopped me in my tracks.

Because the truth is, I don't remember what I was looking at. Something that felt urgent and meant nothing. Probably someone else's life while I missed my own. But I remember what I felt in that moment: Small. Exposed. Guilty.

Because what I said without words, what my actions kept saying day after day, was that this glowing rectangle was more important than you.

And you, tragically, believed me—you believed that the phone was more important than you.

Giuliana, your question didn't just sting. It *split* something open in me.

The worst part is that I can't tell you what I was doing on my phone. Was it email? News? Sports?

It doesn't matter. Because if it's forgettable to me now, it wasn't worth what it cost then. We are all wasting moments on borrowed time, waiting for an end date to start living. We put off the important stuff with lines like: "Let's play it by ear." "Maybe when I have more time." "Tomorrow." "Once things settle down." "When the stars align."

But that's how years disappear. We stack to-do lists like bricks, build walls around our lives, and then wonder why we feel trapped inside them.

Not long after that, I had a night where I couldn't sleep. Not from stress. Not caffeine. Something quieter. A stillness that felt like suffocation. I couldn't fall asleep, and I stared at the ceiling while a strange thought whispered into the silence: What if I went a year without my phone? Not a weekend. Not a detox. A year. No flip phone. No landline. No screen in my pocket at all.

Five minutes later, I stood before the whiteboard in my office. This made no sense on the surface, but total sense where it matters most: my soul. Instead of listing the hundred reasons it wouldn't work, I picked up a marker and wrote two words: What if?

What if I was already sleepwalking? What if your question was the alarm clock? What if this year turns out to be the best thing that ever happened to me?

Because here's the truth: Most people don't change because someone yelled. They change because someone told the truth and made it sound like a question.

Your question, Giuliana, didn't scold me. It invited me. You held up a mirror, and I saw what I hadn't wanted to face: a father distracted from his calling. A man addicted not just to a device, but to being needed, performing, and avoiding silence.

And the silence? That's what scared me the most. Because it carried the questions I didn't want to answer: Am I alive or just awake? Am I present or just near? Am I building a life—or performing one?

That night, the seed was planted. Your question was the water that would nourish it, and it would grow into a new way of living. It made me realize that I needed to make a change.

We're all tempted to wait for the crisis. The diagnosis. The disaster. The dramatic wake-up call.

But maybe it doesn't have to come to that. Maybe it only takes one honest question from someone who sees you. You didn't just see your dad looking at a phone. You saw him missing his life. You asked, "Why?"

That is why your question became holy. It woke something in me that had long been sleeping. I used to think scrolling was harmless. But what I was doing was teaching you what matters. What love looks like. What I choose when no one's watching.

And now I know: Presence isn't proximity. It's attention. It's eye contact and pancake breakfasts. It's hearing the whole story behind the "Why" before bedtime.

Now, when I hear your feet running down the hallway, when your hands reach for mine, when your eyes search my face for proof that I still choose you—I try to answer with more than just words. I try to answer with my life.

Because there are only so many princess wands I'll step on. Only so many invitations to dance in the kitchen. You'll only ask me to look up so many times before you stop expecting me to.

One day, you'll tell a story. I hope it sounds like this: "My dad was *there*."

Not perfect.

Not always calm.

But present.

Listening.

Loving us more than his phone.

And I want you to know, while you're still small enough to crawl into my lap, that question saved me. It brought me home. I am forever grateful to you, Giuliana, for asking it. It's because of your question that I've become a better father and a better person. It brought me home.

That's what this year has been about. Not just quitting something. But choosing something better. *You.*

All my love,
Daddy

What if you don't need a map, just a light?

(DAY 3)

Dear Girls,

I'm not sure how old you'll be when you're holding this book for the first time. Maybe you're still little. Perhaps you're grown. Maybe you're somewhere in between, wondering what comes next.

But I know this: You've found your way here for a reason. This book wasn't written because I had all the answers. It was written because I finally stopped pretending I did.

It began with a question. A decision. A phone turned off for 365 days.

But really, it began with you. Because in the silence that followed, I saw you more clearly than ever. And I saw myself—who I had become and was still becoming. This year broke me open.

And these letters? They're the pieces I gathered, held to the light, and sent forward...for you. They aren't step-by-step instructions. They aren't rules or formulas. They're not even in the "right order."

This book is not a map. Maps promise routes and destinations. But life rarely works that way.

So, instead, I'm giving you a lantern. It won't show you the whole road. But it will light your next step.

Because I've walked through some dark places, girls. And I've felt the fire that melts away who you were, so you can become someone new. I've screamed into the silence. I've knelt in hospital rooms. I've wondered if I could go on. And I did. Not because I was strong. But because love kept whispering: "Stay."

That's why this book exists. Not to impress you. Not to protect you from life. But to prepare you for it.

To say: Yes, it will hurt. Yes, some dreams will break. Yes, some days you'll wonder if joy was ever real. But it was. It is. It lives in your laugh. In the bounce house. In the bedtime stories. In the living-room dance parties. It lives in your questions. In your ache. In your becoming.

If, one day, you find yourself lost or aching or unsure of where to go next...don't panic. Just pick up this book. Turn to any page.

And remember: I was there, too. You were never alone. And the light will always find you again.

All my love,
Daddy

What if I answered every call but still missed myself?

Dear Girls,

Before I ever said I was going without a cell phone, before I wrote a word of this book, I answered every call. Every email. Every ping. Every notification. Every invitation to perform, to achieve, to be seen.

And for most of my adult life, that wasn't optional; it was the job. As a college basketball official, I was tethered to my phone like it was oxygen.

For nearly two decades, I lived out of a suitcase. From October through March, the season ran my life. I was on the road constantly. There were hundreds of flights, rental cars, and hotel lobbies that all started to look the same. Most mornings began at 4:00 a.m., whether I was ready or not. I'd catch the first flight out, drive to the hotel, work the game, and then sometimes head back to a different hotel in a different city. Rinse and repeat. I got good at making it look effortless…precise, polished, professional. But underneath, I was tired. Not just physically, but in a way I didn't know how to name yet. Officiating gave me structure. It gave me identity. It gave me something to chase. And maybe that was part of the appeal. It kept me moving so I didn't have to stop and ask myself why I was running.

Assignments came through it: Weather updates. Travel alerts. Flight bookings. Hotel confirmations. Rental cars. Group texts with partners to sync arrival times and carpool plans.

Every college conference has a supervisor of officials who assigns the games to officials. If a supervisor called you, even in the middle of the night, you answered. Because if you didn't, they'd move on to the next available official.

It wasn't personal. It was just logistics. There were games to fill. In a career that spanned hundreds of thousands of hours, three of those calls were time-sensitive enough to warrant that kind of hypervigilance.

But somewhere in the mix, my brain made a quiet decision without telling me: *Never be unreachable,* just in case. Just in case opportunity knocks and you miss it. Just in case this is your moment, and you don't pick up. Just in case today's the day when the supervisor calls you in the middle of the night and has you change your travel plans. Maybe I was assigned to work a game in Texas but now was needed in West Virginia.

So I stayed on. Always on. Looking back now, it wasn't just

about logistics. It was more about longing and the fear of being forgotten. The fear of being passed over. It was about my need to prove I was worthy of the next thing.

And honestly? That need didn't go away when I turned off the phone. If anything, it got bigger. Because the silence doesn't lie. The silence doesn't distract. The silence doesn't hand you a hit of dopamine for answering a text. The silence asks: Who are you when no one's watching? Who are you when there's no scoreboard?

That's when I started seeing my phone for what it was: not just a device, but a slot machine. It wasn't just a means of communication; it was also a dopamine dispenser. A pocket-sized casino that paid out just often enough to keep me coming back. The vibration. The blue bubble. The "just checking in" email that made me feel relevant.

I wasn't addicted to the phone. I was addicted to the illusion of control. The illusion of importance. The illusion that if I just stayed reachable, I'd never miss my shot.

But here's what I didn't see until much later: I wasn't just checking for updates. I was checking for worth. And somewhere along the way, I realized something I hadn't been able to admit. Not to your mom. Not to my friends. Not even to myself.

I wasn't just retiring from officiating. I was saying goodbye to the version of me who found his value in being precise, productive, and constantly in motion. The man who felt most alive with a whistle in his hand and a packed calendar. The man who knew how to follow rules and earn respect but didn't always know how to sit still with his own feelings. Letting go of that life didn't feel noble. It felt like grief. Like losing a self I had spent years building—one whistle, one game, one flight at a time. I was burying the first version of me. It didn't feel noble. It felt like a loss.

But now, sitting in this stillness, I can finally call it what it was: a necessary death. The death of a man who believed his worth was tied to performance. The death of a schedule that told me who I was. The death of a curated identity that always needed applause to feel real.

I didn't know it at the time. I couldn't name it. I only knew something had to change.

And that's the most challenging part of craving something deeper: You don't always have the words for it. You feel it in your chest. In your sleep. In your silence. Like a longing for something unnamed. Like homesickness for a place you've never been. And now I see it clearly: I couldn't evolve while clinging to the man I used to be.

To keep officiating would've been to keep performing. To keep *knowing who I was*. And maybe what I was craving, what I couldn't verbalize, was the terrifying gift of *not knowing*. The scary, exhilarating, liberating gift of not knowing. Of having to become someone new. Of having to redefine myself without the familiar markers of my past.

That version of me? He had to die so this one could be born. It's a testament to the power of change, a reminder that we can constantly reinvent ourselves.

And maybe that's the deeper invitation in all of this—not to escape life, run from pain, or throw away everything that came before, but to finally let go of the identity that no longer fits. To grieve it. To thank it. To bury it with love. And to rise.

So, no, this didn't start with a heroic idea. It began with loss. A loss I couldn't explain at the time. I just knew something in me was done. Something in me had outgrown the role, the rhythm, the reflex to answer every call. Something in me was craving quiet, craving meaning, craving me.

You see, girls, I answered every call for most of my life. But I nearly missed myself in the process.

This year of turning off my cell phone, turning toward you, turning inward, wasn't about disconnection. It was about resurrection. It was about rising from the ashes of my old self, shedding the layers of performance and expectation, and embracing a new, more authentic version of me.

All my love,
Daddy

What if I had a meth problem?

(**DAY 11**)

Dear Girls,

I wish I had a meth problem. I know how insane that sounds. But hear me out.

If I had come to my family in August 2023 and said, "Hey, I've been hiding this from you for a while now. Meth has become addictive, and I'm unable to get through my day without having it by my side. I think about it as soon as I wake up; it's the first thing I reach for. I think about it as I fall asleep; it's the last thing I put down before bed. It has reached a point where I need to seek professional help. I found the world's most renowned meth rehab facility, and I'm going to enroll in a yearlong treatment plan. While I'm there, they will remove all distractions from the outside world, including my cell phone."

I would've been met with a compassionate urgency if I had said that. No one would have told me I was overreacting. No one would have laughed nervously, shrugged it off, or said, "You think you need to go that far?"

Instead, I would've heard, "We're here for you. Take all the time you need. Do whatever it takes to get well." Because when someone names their addiction with a word like meth, we understand it as dangerous. Desperate. Worthy of intervention.

But I didn't say meth. I said my cell phone. I said I was turning it off for an entire year. Not just deleting a few apps or going on a silent retreat for a weekend. Off. For 365 days. No smartphone. No dumb phone. No burner. No emergency line. Just...off.

Instead of support, I got confusion. Concern. Skepticism. Jokes. Blank stares. A few people thought it was "cool," in the way someone might say skydiving is cool, as long as it's not them falling from the plane.

But most people? The ones I loved the most? They thought I'd lost my mind. And maybe I had. The truth is, I wasn't just addicted to the device. I was addicted to the identity it allowed me to curate. I was addicted to being needed. Addicted to being in control. Addicted to that tiny dopamine drip of a notification, a response, a like. Addicted to the illusion that I was important. Relevant. On top of things. Addicted to avoiding the silence that would ask harder questions.

I thought giving up the phone would be the hard part. But it wasn't. The hard part was what the silence brought up. It was the realization of my loneliness, even with constant connection. It was facing how much I'd outsourced my sense of self to a screen. It was the discomfort my loved ones felt with my choice that made me question myself.

When my loved ones didn't understand, it stung more than I expected. It stung because a part of me had hoped they'd see what I couldn't yet say: that I wasn't just tired...I was soul-tired. I didn't need a weekend off or a mindfulness app. I needed to come back to life—not in the self-help sense, but in the actual sense. I had been running so hard for so long, performing so often for so many, that I'd lost touch with the person underneath it all. What I needed wasn't a break from the noise; it was to be brought back from the dead. And that kind of return doesn't come from rest. It comes from reckoning.

For the first few weeks, I almost went back. Because belonging is addictive, too. Eventually, I stopped asking for permission. I let their doubt be theirs. And I walked into the silence anyway. Because sometimes, what looks like madness to others is the first real moment of sanity you've had in years.

This journey taught me a hundred things, but none more important than this: Right now is the best time to take action. We all whisper it. Those four words that kill dreams slowly: *I'll do that when...* When the timing's right. When the chaos settles. When I feel more ready.

I'm telling you, girls: *I'll do that when* is how people stay numb forever.

So, I started writing you letters. Not because I have the answers. But because I finally stopped waiting to ask the questions.

All my love,
Daddy

What if there's no perfect time to begin?

(DAY 15)

Dear Girls,

If you read this one day and wonder if I thought this whole thing through, I did.

You should know I didn't choose to turn off my phone during some peaceful, slow season. This wasn't a sabbatical on a mountaintop. This wasn't a "gap year" or a midlife luxury with built-in support. This was the worst possible time to do something so drastic.

Let me paint the picture. I had just started a business as an executive coach and keynote speaker. We had both of you at home, under the age of four. Your mom was still mourning the loss of her mother. My dad's health was uncertain. Our world was already stretched thin, and I was about to snap it tighter.

As you know, it came to me not in a brainstorm, but in the middle of the night. June 28, 2023.

I woke up in the dark, heart pounding, thoughts racing. No dream. No thunder. Just that question I couldn't un-hear: "What if you turned your cell phone off for a year?"

I didn't share it with anyone, not even your mom. I didn't write it down. I just turned it over in my head a hundred different ways. I imagined what I'd lose. What I'd gain. How might it work logistically? What would it mean for you? How would your mom take it? How would I handle it?

But the idea stayed, no matter how hard I tried to shake it. Not like a hobby. Like a calling. It felt wild and stupid and sacred. Like I had stumbled on a secret I couldn't unhear. And once I heard it, nothing else felt true. And I'll be honest with you: There were two big reasons I didn't wait until January 1 to start.

I knew that waiting would invite doubt. The longer I sat with the idea, the louder my fear grew. The more time I gave myself, the more opportunity there was for logic to kill it. I wasn't sure why I was doing it other than that I'd had some crazy idea in the middle of the night. It became clear a few weeks in that this idea came from God. It turned into something much more profound than a cute little experiment.

So I didn't wait. On August 6, 2023, the second anniversary of starting my business, I turned off my cell phone. No grand announcement. No social media goodbye. Just a quiet, deliberate click. I sat on the edge of my bed, holding the phone in my hand like it was something alive.

For a second, my thumb hovered over the power button. Not because I was unsure, but because I knew that once I pressed it, I couldn't unpress it. This wasn't a pause. This was a complete stop.

When the screen went black, the silence wasn't just around me; it was also in me. I stood up, walked into my closet, and placed the phone on the shelf next to a stack of shorts. That's where it would stay for the next 365 days. No ritual. No burning sage. Just a man alone in his room, making the smallest move that would change everything.

Before that moment came, I had a conversation I'll never forget. One afternoon, I took your mom on a walk, hoping to share my vision and gain her support. We had the dog with us. It was a bright, sunny day. The air felt calm. I had just finished writing my first children's book, and I was still experiencing the high of putting that out into the world.

"I think I know my next book," I said.

She looked over. Curious. Skeptical.

I looked straight ahead and said, "I'm going to turn off my phone for a year."

Without missing a beat, she said sternly, "Absolutely not." Just like that. One sentence. The door slammed shut. And here's the confusing part: I saw this, even before it started, as something that would be phenomenal for our family in the long run. Even if there were temporary setbacks.

She thought I was walking away. She wasn't cruel. She was scared. Tired. Raw.

Still grieving the loss of her mom only a year prior. And I'll admit this, girls: I wasn't really asking. I'd already made the decision. That's one of my flaws. I'm decisive to a fault. And in a marriage, that's not always a strength. Sometimes, it's a shortcut through someone else's fear.

We finished the walk in silence. Nothing explosive. Nothing dramatic. Just this invisible wall between us. The kind that doesn't yell. It just settles. And still, something in me said: Do it anyway. Not in rebellion. But in obedience to something I didn't fully understand yet.

That's the thing about these moments. They come uninvited. And they rarely come when everything feels calm.

You may face moments like this one day, when your clarity makes someone else uncomfortable. When your *yes* feels like a *no* to someone you love. When the thing that's calling you forward feels like a betrayal to those who don't yet see it. And you'll have to choose. Not between love and purpose. But between postponing your purpose for someone else's comfort or pursuing it with compassion.

I didn't start this journey because it made sense. I started it because something inside me said, *This will change you.* And it did. In every way. In ways I never could have imagined. If somehow, someone had given me a look into the future and shown me everything that would happen over 365 days, I wouldn't have moved forward.

This year didn't leave me with all the answers, but it stripped away every lie I'd been living. And yes, it was lonely. There were moments when I doubted everything. There were nights when I looked at your mom and thought I'd lost her trust.

I knew if I waited for full support, if I waited until things slowed down, if I waited until I had the right words, I would never do this at all.

So, I said yes to turning off my phone and stepping into the unknown. Not sure if my business would be affected. Not sure if relationships would change. Not because I was ready. But because I was awake.

If you're reading this, feeling torn, scared, and like no one gets your crazy ideas, that's not a sign to stop. That's a sign you're on the edge of something real. When the time comes to answer your calling, you don't need permission.

You need truth. And the truth is this: There's no perfect time. Only now.

All my love,
Daddy

What if you're chasing a life you don't even want?

(DAY 21)

Dear Girls,

There's a kind of sickness we don't diagnose. It doesn't leave bruises or break bones. But it wears you down until you forget you're allowed to want something different.

It's the kind of ache that comes from living a life you never really chose.

We do things because we're told they're markers of success.

Buy the house.

Drive the car.

Say yes to the promotion.

Renovate the kitchen.

Smile for the Christmas card like everything's fine.

But beneath the checklist, most of us are quietly wondering, *Why does this still feel empty?*

Before I turned off my phone, I thought I was living with purpose. But in the silence that followed, I realized I was following patterns. Meeting expectations I never paused to question. And I'm not just talking about stuff. I'm talking about identity. I'm talking about meaning. What it means to be a good man. A good father. A whole human being.

Somewhere along the way, success became synonymous with exhaustion. Hustle culture baptized us in the lie that burnout is just part of the deal. Now we trade presence for productivity and call it ambition.

But the most dangerous trade? We give away our time, the one thing we don't get back, for things we stop noticing two weeks after buying them.

You know what's wild? If I were to walk into a grocery store at 10:00 a.m. holding a bottle of whiskey, someone would stop me. They'd ask if I was okay. But if I walk in glued to my phone, dead-eyed and distracted, no one bats an eye. Because distraction is normal. Disconnection is accepted. But our souls still notice.

The low-level hum of discontent inside you? The ache in your chest when everything's "fine"? That's your spirit saying, "This isn't the life you were made for."

You don't need to sell everything and vanish. But you do need to get honest.

Ask yourself: Whose life am I living? Whose dream am I chasing?

I realized I was sprinting toward a life that looked impressive on paper but left me feeling hollow in person. The phone going dark didn't fix everything. But it did remove the noise long enough for the truth to get through.

I don't want a life that looks good only in photos. I want a life that feels good even in silence. One where I'm fully here. Fully human. Fully mine.

Please understand that I am not against cell phones; I am merely against the burden of regret, which may or may not surface for many years to come. The kind that sneaks in late, after you've built the whole house and then realized it was never your blueprint.

Every blueprint should come with a question at the top: What if you're chasing a life you don't even want?

I stopped long enough to ask. And now, I'm building something slower. Something truer. Something I hope you'll recognize not by how it looks, but by how it feels.

All my love,
Daddy

What if you're watching me die slowly?

(DAY 26)

Dear Girls,

You were starting your bedtime routine. Pajamas. Toothbrushes. Stories waiting on your pillows.

You had no idea that your dad was quietly unraveling.

I've had four panic attacks in my life. The first three came in my freshman year at Dayton when I was eighteen. I remember being strapped to a stretcher in a trauma bay, listening to doctors yell, "Chest X-ray, *stat!*" like I was in a scene from *Grey's Anatomy.*

They ran every test. Nothing was wrong. Except everything was. Stress. Fear. Pressure I didn't know how to name.

That was twenty years ago.

The fourth panic attack? That happened just a few weeks ago, right before I decided to turn off my phone for a year.

That night before our bedtime routine, I imagined a phone call. A big opportunity. A speaking gig in the form of a $15,000 check. It came from a friend of a client. One of those "right place, right time" miracles.

But I wouldn't have a phone. I wouldn't get the voicemail. The moment would disappear.

And just like that, my body revolted. Palms sweating. Chest tightening. My heartbeat turned into a stampede; I couldn't slow it down. And through the chaos, one thought rose like a scream: *Don't let your girls see you die.* Over and over. Like a drumbeat. Like a warning. Like a promise I didn't know I'd made.

I left your room and told your mom I needed to check something. I walked outside. Stumbled, really. My vision blurred. My body buzzed with panic. And I thought, *This might be it. I will collapse in the backyard, and your mom will find me.*

I don't remember how long I stayed out there. But I breathed. Deeply. Slowly. I kept telling myself: *You're okay. This is mental.* And eventually, my body believed me.

I walked back upstairs like nothing had happened. But something had. And girls, this is the part I need you to know: "Don't let your girls see you die" haunted me. Not because of a single moment, but because of all the moments. I was dying slowly by ignoring what lit me up.

I kept pretending not to hear. That panic attack wasn't about a missed phone call. It was about a missed calling. One I'd been shrinking from. One I was too scared to say out loud. Scared to risk. Scared to disappoint. Scared to want something *bigger* than safe.

But that night, struggling to fall asleep, I knew. No, I decided. I'd rather miss fifty gigs than the chance to show you what *living* looks like. I don't want to just tell you to chase your dreams. I want you to see me do it. Even when it's messy. Even when no one claps. Even when I don't know where I'll land.

That panic attack didn't take anything from me. It gave me something. Clarity. Conviction. And a truth I'll carry with me forever. The bravest thing you can do is refuse to die—not all at once, but slowly, by abandoning who you're here to become—in front of the people you love.

So, girls, this year is for you. But it's also for me.

All my love,
Daddy

Can you be safe
without being certain?

Dear Girls,

Giuliana, you asked me if you could sleep with the light on tonight. "There might be monsters," you whispered. You didn't scream it. You didn't cry. You just said it like it was a possibility you'd quietly been calculating all day. Like the idea of monsters wasn't outrageous, just reasonable.

I didn't laugh. Because I get it. I sat on the edge of your bed, rubbed your back, and told you there were no monsters in the closet or under the bed. "You're safe," I said, and I meant it.

But after I tucked you in, turned off the closet light, and walked down the stairs...I wished someone would say the same thing to me. Because there are nights I still believe in monsters, too. Not the kind hiding in dark corners. The kind I can't name because they live in the future. The "what ifs."

What if something happens to one of you girls?

What if I miss a crisis because I don't have my phone?

What if I ruin something I can't fix?

What if this whole thing...the silence, the stillness, the leaving behind of all I once relied on to feel important—what if it's all just a big mistake?

This is what I'm noticing now that I'm at thirty-nine days without a phone:

People don't really ask me how it's going without a phone. Not really. They ask, "Aren't you scared?" At first, I thought they meant being scared of missing a text or getting lost without GPS. But that's not it. They're asking: "Aren't you scared of the unknown? Aren't you scared of the dark?"

We reassure our kids that there are no monsters in the closet. But who reassures us? Who tells the adults it's safe to sleep? Kids imagine the monster under the bed. Grown-ups imagine the monster in the future. Same imagination. Same fear. Same ache for control.

Here's the truth I'm starting to believe, slowly, like a candle flickering to life:

The future isn't real. Only now is. Only this moment, sitting on the edge of your bed. Only the sound of your breath slowing as I hum you a song I barely remember. Only the courage to whisper, "Keep the light on," when you feel afraid.

Sometimes, I think the bravest thing we can do in this world is to live like children who trust their father when he says, "You're safe." Not because we're guaranteed a pain-free life. Not because the light will stay on forever. But because love is here. In the now. And love is enough to make the monsters shrink.

All my love,
Daddy

What if disconnection is mostly just inconvenient at first?

$$\text{DAY 46}$$

Dear Girls,

Three haircuts. One week. Zero completed on time. That's how this journey started.

Let me explain. During the first week of my phone-free year, I had a haircut scheduled for Thursday. I showed up, ready to get cleaned up, only to be met with the look—equal parts pity, apology, and panic. "We're so sorry, Tommy. We tried to call and text you. Your stylist is out sick."

Not a big deal. They rescheduled me for Saturday.

Saturday came. I walked in. Same look. Same apology.

"She's still sick. We tried calling and texting you."

This time, I smiled. Shrugged. I considered explaining the no-phone-for-a-year thing, but I just said, "No big deal."

They set a new date, and I finally got the haircut a few days later. Three appointments. One actual cut. And honestly, I couldn't help but laugh all the way home. It was like a comedy of errors, but it wasn't tragic in the end. It was telling, though.

Here's what I started to notice, especially in those first thirty days without a cell phone: Disconnection doesn't dismantle your life. It just...inconveniences it.

That's what vanishes first—not connection, but convenience. The tiny efficiencies. The shortcuts. The go-betweens. And when those are gone? You don't fall apart. You get a little slower. A little more deliberate.

Your mom came along with the project, but I agreed on one rule: She wouldn't become my secretary. No texts on my behalf. No quick "just this once" calls. If I chose this path, I needed to walk it. So when I hit my first real snag, a forgotten two-factor authentication step while trying to pay a bill online, I heard the internal whisper: "Just turn it on. No one will know."

But I would know. And I've learned if you betray yourself for a shortcut, it never stays quiet.

So, I drove to the bank. Waited in line. Explained—not once, not twice, but three times—that I didn't lose my phone; I'd just decided not to use it. They looked at me like I was speaking Morse code. It took over two hours to verify who I was.

The following week, at the car dealership, a similar encounter: "No, you can't text me when it's ready." Same look. Same awkward silence. Same lesson.

The modern world isn't built for waiting. But once you start, you realize how much you've been missing. You hear the fizzing of the soda machine. The door creaking open. A mother whispering encouragement to her toddler.

It's not transcendence. But it is presence. That's what I want you to understand, girls.

Not every part of this journey was profound. Some parts of this journey weren't very pleasant. There were moments of frustration, awkwardness, and inconvenience. But here's the truth I uncovered: We avoid chasing the future we want because of the discomfort it causes in the present.

We choose easy over meaningful. Fast over deep. But sometimes, the "hassle" is the gateway.

Living without a phone forced me to slow down to be here. And once I leaned into it, I found something I didn't know I'd lost.

If one day you decide to do something bold, or weird, or wildly inconvenient, expect the awkward. Expect missed voicemails and puzzled faces. Expect two-hour waits at the bank trying to prove you are who you say you are. Expect the silence between songs.

It might feel strange at first. Maybe even stupid. But give it time. The discomfort is temporary, but the rewards are eternal. It'll start to feel honest. It'll start to feel like you.

Maybe, just maybe, that's the hidden truth: Sometimes you have to lose the convenience to recover the connection.

Even if it takes three appointments to get a haircut. It's worth it.

All my love,
Daddy

What if strength isn't what I thought it was?

(DAY 50)

Dear Girls,

I used to think strength meant silence. That being a man meant being composed, controlled, and unbothered. That real leaders didn't flinch. That dads didn't cry. That husbands always held it together. That showing emotion was a weakness. That needing help was something you quietly outgrew.

No one taught me those things outright. It was quieter than that. It was learned in the space between the lines—the way men made jokes about crying, the way people changed the subject when the air got heavy, how quickly we praised toughness, and how rarely we praised tenderness. I wore my learned silence like armor. And it served me in some places.

As a basketball referee, you're taught to be calm in chaos. You blow the whistle even when the crowd hates you for it. You take the yelling. You take the second-guessing. You don't feel.

You manage. There's no room for tears on the hardwood. No space for "I'm not okay."

I started bringing the whistle home along the way without even realizing it.

In my personal life, I wore that same invisible jersey. Stoic. Unshaken. In control. I thought that was what made me dependable. I thought that was what love looked like: showing up, never falling apart.

But here's what I've learned in the silence: That kind of strength? It only looks good from a distance. Up close, it's a wall. It can sound like composure when someone needs your tenderness. It can look like "holding it together" when what's needed is for you to fall apart with someone in the middle of their pain.

Being "strong" made me good at my job. But it made me a stranger to myself. When I turned off my phone and stepped away from the endless notifications, praise loops, and crisis-managing, the mask didn't know where to go anymore. The version of me that knew how to be needed didn't know who he was without someone needing him.

That's when I tried something I'd been avoiding for years: therapy. I didn't go because something was broken, but because something was buried. And I was tired of pretending I didn't need anything.

I owe that step to my friend Tim. He never pushed. Never gave me a lecture. He talked honestly about how therapy helped him find language for things he didn't know how to name. How it softened him. Strengthened him—not by fixing, but by freeing. So, I made the appointment. On a Tuesday afternoon, I parked outside the two-story beige building and sat in the car for a while. Engine off. Heart loud. I kept telling myself, *You're just going in to talk.* But it felt like walking into a gym for working out muscles I'd never trained.

The lobby was small. Quiet. Muted earth tones. A bowl of those mints no one ever takes. An assortment of herbal teas, like maybe warmth could convince you to open up. Like peppermint could help release something that's been locked tight for years.

The receptionist smiled. I gave her my name. She handed me a clipboard. For a moment, it hit me: *I don't even know how to say what I'm feeling. What if I don't cry? What if I do?*

The chairs were soft but too upright, like they were built to hold your discomfort just enough to keep you from running. I took a few deep breaths and waited to be called.

When I finally entered the therapist's office, we exchanged a few pleasantries, small talk that felt too small. And then came the question that opened a door I didn't even know was closed: "So, what brings you in?"

I said something truer than I'd said in a long time: "I don't know. I just didn't want to keep doing it like *this.*" A chance to say something more honest than "I'm fine."

Therapy didn't give me answers. But it gave me better questions. Questions that gently pulled me toward the version of myself I had buried under years of applause and performance and perfectly managed moments. It helped me see how I'd mistaken retreat for strength. How I pulled away when life got loud. How I let the world's definition of masculinity shrink the range of what I thought I was allowed to feel.

And girls, let me tell you something I never heard growing up: Crying isn't failure. Feeling doesn't make you fragile. Needing help doesn't make you weak. Vulnerability isn't the opposite of strength; it's the doorway into it. One day, someone might say "man up" like it's a badge of honor.

I hope you remember this: A real man sits on the therapy couch. A real man apologizes. A real man listens. A real man says, "I don't know," and keeps showing up anyway.

I used to think strength was having the answers. Now, I know it's the courage to keep asking better questions. I used to think strength was control. Now, I know it means surrender. I used to think strength was keeping it all together. Now, I believe that real strength is letting it fall apart when it needs to and still choosing to stay.

Girls, I want you to grow up knowing that your softness is sacred. That your anger deserves a voice. That your fear isn't a flaw. That your tenderness isn't an inconvenience. That your tears aren't something to hide.

If the world ever tells you to "be strong" in the way it once told me to hold it in, toughen up, smile through the ache, I hope you'll have the courage to ask: Strong for who? Strong for what? And what is that strength costing me?

The world doesn't need more people who look strong. It needs more people who are willing to be honest. And if you ever feel like you're breaking, I want you to know: I've broken, too. And I'm still here. Not because I held it together, but because I finally learned how to let go.

All my love,
Daddy

What happens when you stop being available?

DAY 56

Dear Girls,

There's a particular kind of violence in always being available. But nobody calls it that. They call it being nice. They call it being dependable. They call it being "a good person."

For a long time, I wore those labels like armor. I thought love looked like readiness. I thought the sacrifice was proof of worth. I thought picking up every call, answering every text, and saying "yes" when my chest was screaming "no" meant I was dependable, good, and safe to love.

But it wasn't goodness. It was slow erosion. It was death by a thousand tiny self-betrayals. Whenever I laughed at a joke that wasn't funny, agreed to plans that made my skin itch, and stayed on a call I wanted to end, I silently abandoned myself.

Packing a suitcase. Moving farther and farther out of my own life. When I turned off my phone, it was the first time I barricaded the door. And I swear to you, girls, I could hear the world clawing at it. At first, it sounded like concern: "Are you okay?" "Where did you go?" "Why are you being so weird lately?"

Soon, the concern curdled into accusation: "You've changed." "You're selfish now." "You think you're better than us?"

No. I hadn't gotten better. I had gotten empty. And when you finally realize how hollow you've become from giving yourself away, you stop offering pieces of yourself like free samples at a grocery store.

Girls, listen close: People will guilt you for growing. They will shame you for protecting your peace. They will resent that they can no longer yank your strings and make you dance. Their resentment isn't about you. It's about them losing control.

And it will hurt. It will feel like pulling barbed wire from your ribcage. You will question yourself. You will wonder if you're being cruel. You will ache for the old warmth, even when you know it burned you every time you touched it. But you must keep going. Because here's the blood truth: If you are available to everyone, you disappear from yourself. Your life becomes rented out to the highest bidder.

Your worth is not measured by how fast you answer, how quickly you fold, and how much of yourself you're willing to auction off for scraps of approval. One day, if you aren't careful, you'll look in the mirror and realize you no longer recognize the stranger staring back at you. Only a body shaped by everyone else's needs. Only a mouth that's spent a lifetime saying words that didn't belong to it.

When you stop being available, you stop being predictable. You stop being a vending machine for emotional snacks. And it terrifies people. Because now, they have to face the uncomfortable truth: Maybe they didn't love you. They loved your compliance. Your easy "yes." Your access. And when the "yes" dried up, so did the false connections. You find out who's real when you disappear for a while. You find out who notices your silence and honors it. You find out who shows up without a withdrawal slip in hand.

Girls, the world will call you cold when you refuse to be consumed. That's okay. The world will call you arrogant when you stop explaining your boundaries. That's okay. The world will call you difficult when you refuse to set yourself on fire to keep other people warm. That's okay. Your peace is not up for negotiation. Your soul is not a public utility. You owe no one your exhaustion. You owe no one your erosion. You owe no one your life. Not even me.

One day, someone will knock on your heart, and every old reflex in you will stir. You'll feel the pull to open wide and say, "Take whatever you need." I hope you hesitate. I hope you pause long enough to ask yourself: "Is this love, or is this a robbery disguised as a hug?"

Because you, my daughters, are not a public park. You are a sacred country with guarded borders. And anyone who deserves to enter will be patient enough to earn it. Hold your silence like it's holy. Let your "no" be as sacred as your "yes."

Sometimes, the most loving thing you can do—for yourself and for others—is to be gloriously, unapologetically unavailable. Because your heart was never meant to be a revolving door. Treat it like Fort Knox. Entry requires a thorough background check, and even then, not everyone makes it inside.

And if they don't? Lock the gate behind you.

All my love,
Daddy

What if the hardest voices are the ones you need the most?

(DAY 59)

Dear Girls,

I remember seeing the look on your mom's face that morning. The kind of look where no one has to say a word because their expression says it all.

I almost turned my phone on that day. It was the day we lost John Adams, my first mentor in officiating. I hadn't broken my commitment, but grief has a way of testing resolve.

I felt it everywhere. In my chest. In my stomach. In my hands, itching to pick up the phone. I wanted to call one of my good friends, Tim, John's son. I wanted to tell him how much my heart hurt. How much his dad meant to me. How much this loss was echoing inside places I hadn't visited in a long time. But then I remembered a line I once heard entrepreneur Jesse

Itzler say: "When a friend experiences a loss, you don't call. You show up."

So I did. I got in the car and showed up. Because sometimes, your presence is more potent than anything you could say. It's about being there—not just in words, but in actions. I remember walking into John's house. His wife and Tim were sitting in the kitchen. The silence echoed. The air was heavy with grief, and I could feel the weight of the loss.

I met John almost twenty years ago, in a suite at a Pacers game. He wasn't warm and fuzzy (this is one of his traits I would come to love and respect over the next twenty years). He wasn't trying to win me over. But in less than thirty seconds, he said nineteen words that would change everything: "The only thing I can give you is an opportunity. What you do with it is up to you."

And from that moment, he became more than a professional contact. He became my mentor. He was the one who opened the door to officiating. Who taught me how to lead without needing applause. Who gave me feedback that wasn't always easy to hear but was always designed to make me better.

If I'm being honest, I didn't always like his words. But I never doubted his heart. Because John didn't say what you wanted to hear; he said what you needed to know. That's what a good mentor does. We live in a world where too many people flatter, and not enough people sharpen. Where comfort is confused for kindness, and challenge is seen as an attack. But John didn't nod just to keep the peace. He challenged your thinking. He didn't perform politeness. He practiced precision. And if he loved you, he told you the truth even when it hurt. Especially when it hurt. Because growth often comes from discomfort.

When I retired from officiating, a decision I didn't take lightly, I dreaded calling him. I thought he might see it as giving up. That I had quit on something he helped start. But instead, he gave me grace. He listened. He asked thoughtful questions. And then he gave me the longest phone call we'd ever had. Not because he needed to process it, but because he wanted me to know that his support wasn't conditional.

That moment, that unexpected tenderness, meant more to me than any championship assignment ever could. Because that's when I realized something I want you both to remember: Real mentorship isn't about being impressive to someone. It's about them investing in you.

A few months before John passed, we were driving somewhere together when he told me the cancer had come back. He said it with that same blunt honesty I'd come to expect. No dramatics. No fishing for pity. Just facts. But I felt like I had been punched in the chest.

That night, I came home and finally did something I'd been pro-crastinating for three years. I wrote him the thank-you note I had always meant to write. Not because I had the perfect words, but because I didn't want to carry the weight of "maybe one day." I thanked him for the truth. For the guidance. For seeing something in me before I ever saw it in myself. And I didn't wait until the funeral to express my gratitude. I got to tell him while he was still here.

Girls, that's something I want you to carry with you forever: Don't wait until the funeral to say the things that matter. Say them now, while the person is still close enough to hear. Mentors like John are rare. They don't coddle. They don't flatter. They don't clap when you're playing it safe. They show up and speak up. They challenge your thinking not because they want to prove something, but because they want to pull something out of you. They won't always agree with you. But they'll always want the best for you. And that distinction matters. Because in a world obsessed with likes and shares and curated affirmation, the voices that challenge you are often the ones that love you the most.

I miss John. I miss his wisdom. I miss his guidance. I miss how he didn't sugarcoat the truth just because it was easier to swallow. And I wish I could call him to say thank you one more time. But that's the beautiful ache of a great mentor. They leave fingerprints on your soul that never wash away.

Girls, if you're lucky enough to find someone who sees your potential before you do, who holds you to a higher standard than you hold yourself, who loves you enough to be honest when it's easier to stay quiet... Hold onto them. Honor them. And don't make them guess how much they matter. Tell them now. Write the letter. Show up.

Because love doesn't always look like flattery. Sometimes, it looks like feedback. Sometimes, it sounds like the truth. Sometimes, it hurts before it heals. And sometimes, it arrives in the form of a mentor who doesn't care about your comfort because they're too committed to your growth.

All my love,
Daddy

What if silence cuts the deepest?

$$\boxed{\text{DAY 63}}$$

Dear Girls,

Some days, I feel like I'm walking around with my insides exposed. Not in a grotesque, horror-movie kind of way, but in a way that means I finally stopped pretending everything inside me was in the right place.

Most people live on the surface. It's easier that way. Smiles are cheaper than surgeries, and small talk is safer than soul work. But going a year without a cell phone has this way of peeling you back, one layer at a time. Like life held up a mirror and said, "Let's stop pretending. Let's see what's really going on underneath." I didn't expect to spend this year doing an autopsy. But that's what it became. An emotional postmortem of me.

It started with questions I didn't want to ask. Questions I had used my phone to outrun. But when the distractions died, the silence got loud.

The silence started asking: What are you breathing life into? What's living in you that should've died long ago? Which poisons are you filtering out—and which ones are you just swallowing? Are you actually living, or are you just digesting things that help you stay numb?

This is what I mean when I say I performed an autopsy. I didn't need a scalpel. Just honesty.

First, I found my pride. It was right there in the chest cavity, beating faster anytime someone questioned my choices. I wanted to be right more than I wanted to be well. That's when I realized I hadn't given up my phone to prove something to the world. I'd given it up because I didn't know how to put down my ego.

Then came the lungs. You'd think after removing so much noise, breathing would become easier. But no. I found I'd been inhaling expectations and exhaling disappointment. I was trying to breathe life into a version of myself that looked good on paper but never felt like home. And that tension? It collapsed me. Quietly. Slowly. Almost beautifully.

Moving lower, I found bitterness curled up in my liver like it had been living rent-free for years. It turns out that some emotions don't just pass through you. They hide until you stop long enough to feel where they've settled.

I didn't expect to find fear in my stomach, but there it was, tangled up in everything I consumed—not just food, but ideas, images, and opinions. I'd been feeding my comfort more than my soul. Growth tastes like discomfort, and I hadn't acquired the appetite.

I thought I'd find clarity by the time I reached the brain. But no. I found overthinking. Worry masquerading as wisdom. Planning as a disguise for control. It turns out my head had been running the show, but my heart had been whispering, *I'm still bleeding.*

Girls, I know this all sounds heavy. Maybe even a little graphic. But I share it because I want you to know that true healing starts with radical honesty. Not performance. Not perfection. Just the courage to open yourself up and take a look inside.

We spend so much time trying to *appear* okay. But wholeness doesn't come from appearances. It comes from presence. And presence starts with being willing to ask, *What worries me more: what the world would see, or what I might discover?* I know now that the fear of discovery is where freedom begins.

So, here's my challenge: Don't wait for a crisis or chaos to start your autopsy. Start while you're still breathing. Still moving. Still able to make changes. Don't numb what needs naming.

If it helps, remember that sometimes the deepest kind of love we can offer ourselves is to look in the mirror and say, "Let's find out what's *really* in there."

All my love,
Daddy

What if becoming yourself means being misunderstood?

$$\boxed{\text{DAY 70}}$$

Dear Girls,

Though many never recognize it, there's a moment in every person's life when the nest feels too small.

At first, the nest is everything. It's safe. It's familiar. It holds you. It feeds you. But over time, if you pay attention, you'll start to feel something in your chest that says: This isn't it. Not anymore.

It's not that the nest was bad. It's just that you've outgrown it.

No bird has ever learned to fly by staying in the nest. That was the tension I felt this year: the quiet, almost invisible ache of outgrowing something that once fit perfectly. It didn't happen because I stopped loving my life. It happened because I started listening to the part of me that wanted more. More depth. More honesty. More presence.

That's when I realized something no one had ever said out loud: Your growth will make some people uncomfortable. And when it does, your first instinct will be to shrink. To apologize for the way you've changed. To keep pretending you fit in the places you've outgrown. To tone it down so you don't get left out.

Here's what I want you to know: You are not obligated to stay the same to make others feel safe. I used to think if I explained it better—if I could articulate my journey just right—then people would nod and say, "Wow, that's beautiful. I get it now." But some people won't get it. Not because they're bad or wrong, but because your growth confronts their own stillness.

When I turned off my phone, I thought the challenge would be the silence. But it wasn't. The hardest part was being misunderstood. When people asked, "Why would you do that?" I didn't always have the perfect answer. The truth is, it wasn't about the phone. It was about the person I could feel I was becoming.

That version of me needed space. He needed stillness. He needed silence so sacred that no one else could interrupt it. That kind of self-growth? It threatens people. When you evolve, it forces others to ask: Am I evolving too? Or have I settled?

In the silence, I realized I've done a lot right. I've built a life. I've stayed loyal. I've achieved things others dream about.

I still felt something. That slow restlessness beneath the surface.

The whisper you keep silencing with one more meeting, one more scroll, one more numbing habit.

You don't need another podcast or another book or another system. You need permission. To leave the nest. To become. To take one small step toward who you were created to be—even if it means being misunderstood.

This isn't about rebellion. It's not about making noise. It's about becoming someone you respect when no one's looking.

If that means people don't recognize you anymore? Let them stare. You weren't born to be understood by everyone. You were born to become someone your kids will watch one day and say, "That's what courage looks like."

Girls, if one day people ask you what your dad was like, I hope you say: "He wasn't perfect. But he never stopped growing."

The truth is that growth doesn't require understanding. It requires integrity. The willingness to walk the path, even if you walk it alone. If your journey makes others nervous, love them anyway.

Don't stop moving. Don't wait for consensus to take flight. Your journey is yours. You don't need anyone's approval to soar. Don't clip your wings so someone else doesn't feel left behind. Your life is a testimony, not a negotiation.

Let them misunderstand you. Let them question your choices. Let them call it weird, extreme, or unnecessary. And then let your peace speak for itself. Because one day, someone will say, "You've changed." And you'll smile and realize that's the greatest compliment another person can give you—not because you're trying to be better than anyone, but because by staying the same, you started to feel like you were dishonoring who you were made to be.

So fly, even if no one claps. Grow, even if no one gets it. Become, even if it costs you comfort.

All my love,
Daddy

Why are you still looking back there?

(DAY 77)

Dear Girls,

I was in the gym, mid-set, with sweat sliding down my face. The weight in front of me was enough to make me strain but not enough to keep me focused. Somewhere between reps five and six, I did the thing most guys do: I turned my head. Just slightly. Just long enough to clock the dude across the room and catch the numbers on the sides of the dumbbells he was curling. Bigger than mine. And just like that, my attention left my body and jumped into someone else's lane.

I wasn't thinking about my breath anymore. I wasn't thinking about my form. I was thinking about whether I was stronger than that guy. Whether he was stronger than me. Whether anyone *saw*.

And here's the truth: That single glance backward carried more weight than the barbell I was holding. Because it didn't come from curiosity. It came from insecurity.

That little turn of the head? It was a mirror. And I didn't like what it showed me. It showed me how much of my energy still goes into comparison. Into competition. Into constantly asking, "Am I enough *yet*?"

In that moment, something in me whispered, clearer than anything I'd heard in a long time: *You can't become who you're meant to be if you're always looking over your shoulder.*

That's when I thought about the box scores. It was a Saturday night about a year ago, and three years since I'd stepped off the court and retired as a college basketball official. I was sitting alone in the kitchen while the rest of the house had already surrendered to sleep. The dishwasher hummed like a lullaby in the background, but I wasn't tired. Or maybe I was and just didn't want to feel it. I opened my laptop to pull up scores from that night's college basketball games. I told myself I was just curious. I told myself it would only take twenty seconds. And there it was: the stat sheet.

I didn't care who won. I didn't care how many points were scored. I wasn't there for the alley-oops or the buzzer-beaters. My eyes went straight to the bottom, where three names were printed in small font: the referees. That's all I was really there for.

Right on cue, those two old emotions showed up like toxic friends who knew how to let themselves in without knocking: Jealousy and Judgment.

"That guy? I'm better than him. I should be working that game."

My jaw tightened. My stomach curled in that familiar way it used to before a big game, but now, there was no game to prepare for. Just a phantom ache in the place where ambition used to live.

I closed the laptop, but the comparison stayed open. It lingered. Like a voice behind me, whispering that I'd fallen behind.

It had been three years since I put on a striped shirt, yet I kept checking those box scores like a man returning to a breakup scene, scrolling through his ex's social media. Hoping to see something. Anything. Maybe they missed me. Perhaps they didn't. What was I even looking for?

I could've given you a hundred surface-level answers to explain why I looked at the box scores. Curiosity. Nostalgia. Wanting to know "who's where." But none of those were the truth. They were just rationalizations, little lies dressed up as logic.

The truth? I was stuck. Still trying to measure my worth by numbers that never tell the whole story.

You won't find character in a box score. You won't see the guy who set the perfect screen to get his teammate open. You won't see who dove headfirst for a loose ball or who stayed after practice to cheer up the kid who missed a free throw. You won't see integrity in a stat line. You won't see growth. You won't see grace. The box score is BS. Not just because it leaves out the soul of the game, but because it became a symbol for something much darker in me: my need to remain in the game. I feared that I no longer mattered because I wasn't listed anymore. It's hard to see where you're going when you keep looking at where you've been.

That's what God whispered to me one morning in prayer after weeks of asking Him the same thing: "God, please continue to introduce me to who I'm *becoming* in your eyes. Please point out anything in me that isn't serving you and is holding me back."

And He did. He showed me that every time I looked back, I was missing what was happening right now, in front of me, around me, within me. The man I had once been was still clinging to a title. The man I was becoming was learning to let go of it. Bitterness is a sneaky thief.

It doesn't show up all at once. It trickles in. Through a stat line. Through a side glance. Through a whisper that says, "You're not enough anymore."

But gratitude? Gratitude is a sword. It cuts through all that noise.

I started asking myself: Is this making me a better dad? A better husband? A better speaker? And if the answer was no, I walked away. You don't have to care about basketball to get this.

Someday, you'll have your own version of the box score. You'll compare your life to someone else's highlight reel. You'll scroll through someone's perfect vacation, relationship, and career, and you'll feel something heavy settle in your chest. That's your moment. That's your crossroads.

Don't chase the numbers. Don't measure your worth in stats. And don't mistake visibility for value.

Remember, girls, the things that matter most—faith, love, character, quiet courage—don't show up on the scoreboard. But they *do* show up. They show up in how you treat people when no one's watching. In the grace you give yourself when you fail. In the quiet yes to growth, when it would be easier to stay the same.

If you ever forget that, girls, just know: I did, too. But I'm learning to turn around less. And lean in more.

All my love,
Daddy

What if the silence wasn't the point?

DAY 81

Dear Girls,

The morning it happened, everything felt ordinary. We'd gone to church. We were supposed to head to the zoo with your cousins. It was a simple Sunday, the kind of day you don't think to remember until everything shifts. We had just finished lunch when it started. First came the dizziness. Then, tingling in my fingers. Then, that slow, suffocating tightening in my chest. I thought maybe I could shake it off. I've had panic attacks before. I've powered through before.

But this felt different. Heavier. I walked upstairs to lie down and see if it would pass. It didn't. I got up and walked downstairs. Walked past where you two were sitting at the kitchen table. And I placed myself between you and your mom. Calm. Measured. Rehearsed. Like I had trained for this moment my whole life—not as a referee on the court, but as your dad. I looked your mom in the eyes and said the words I never imagined I'd say: "Stay calm; I don't want to scare the girls. I need you to call 911. I think I'm having a heart attack."

In that moment, I wasn't afraid of the pain. I was afraid of you seeing it. I turned to you and smiled. I told you Daddy wasn't feeling great and that I might see the doctor, and maybe we'd hit the zoo later. I didn't kiss you goodbye. I didn't say, "I love you." I walked toward the garage, took your mom's phone, and started pacing.

I described my symptoms to the 911 operator—pressure, tingling, shortness of breath—and at the very end of that call, I said something I hope you'll remember: "Please ask them to cut the sirens. I don't want my girls to hear them."

I couldn't stomach the thought of you running outside and seeing your hero strapped to a stretcher. I wanted to shield you from the sound of fear. But inside? I was drowning in it.

The EMTs arrived. I climbed onto the gurney. They gave me baby aspirin and nitroglycerin and asked me how bad the pain was. "It's a twelve," I said. "It feels like I'm at the bottom of a pile, and no one can hear me yelling for them to get off."

Once in the back of the ambulance, I remember hearing one of the paramedics say, "Thirty-nine-year-old male. Complaining of chest pain." That's when it hit me: I wasn't invincible. And I wasn't promised more time.

Life, as we know, can be unpredictable. But in that unpredictability, we find our resilience. I don't remember much of the ride to the hospital; it was all a blur, the floating feeling of an out-of-body experience. But what I do remember, what is seared into my spirit, is what happened when we got to the hospital.

They didn't have a room for me. I was parked in a hallway. Pain mounting. Fear rising in the middle of the chaos, with doctors screaming orders and nurses standing around the hospital bed. I specifically remember something our pastor, CJ, said in a recent sermon: "Life, at some point, is going to jolt you. What's in you will come out of you regardless of who is around you. When that happens, we have three choices: we can go inward, outward, or upward."

I tried everything I knew. I tried to go *inward*. To calm my breath like I'd done a thousand times on the court. That didn't work.

I tried to go *outward*. I begged. I shouted for help. I looked around and saw no one meeting my eyes. That didn't work, either.

Finally, I went upward. I stopped fighting. I said, "God, I don't know how to talk to You. I don't know what I'm supposed to say. But if You're real, I need help." And in that moment, I felt a comfort that I can't quite explain—a comfort that only faith can provide.

Right there, in a hospital hallway, hooked up to monitors and IVs, still unsure if my heart would keep beating, something changed. The pain didn't disappear, but the panic did. A strange calm swept over me. I didn't know if I was dying. But I knew I wasn't alone.

A few hours later, as I was still hooked up to the EKG and under close monitoring, a room became available. Once they got me settled, I asked for some paper and a pen from one of the nurses, and I began jotting down everything swirling in my mind. I kept hearing a phrase in my head, over and over: *Second Corinthians. Second Corinthians. Second Corinthians.*

I knew this was in the Bible, but I didn't even know what it was. I couldn't have quoted a single verse. I had a Bible at home but didn't grow up reading it. I didn't know the difference between a psalm and a proverb. But I wrote it down: *Second Corinthians.*

Eventually, the tests came back. My troponin levels, a marker for heart damage, were elevated, and then they dropped. It might have been a mild heart attack. It might have been something else. The doctors and nurses still didn't know for sure. More tests would be needed to rule out any further damage. But I do know this: That day became the beginning of something bigger than a medical scare.

That day was the start of a profound spiritual journey for me. It was a wake-up call, a reminder of the fragility of life and the importance of faith. It was a moment when I truly felt the presence of a higher power, a reassurance that I was not alone in my struggle.

After a few more hours of poking and prodding, I was released and instructed to follow up with a cardiologist.

The next morning, I opened a dusty Bible and flipped to that section. Second Corinthians. Here's what I found: Second Corinthians is a letter in the Bible written by a man named Paul to his friends in a place called Corinth. Paul wanted to remind them that God is always with us, especially when we're feeling sad or weak. He told them that even though we're not perfect, God can still use us to do great things. Paul also said he was sorry if his last letter was a little tough, but it was because he cared about them. He encouraged them to be kind and generous, especially to people who need help. Most of all, he reminded them to keep trying to do the right thing, even when it's hard, and to focus on what is good and true.

Girls, I didn't turn off my phone because I wanted to become holy. I turned it off because I couldn't hear my own heart anymore. In that hospital bed, I finally did. This was never just about silence. This was about surrender.

That's what Second Corinthians is all about, too. Not the strength of performance, but the strength of weakness. Not avoiding the pain, but letting it lead you to something truer. Not fixing yourself, but letting yourself be held. That day, my body gave out for a bit and my soul woke up. And what I heard in that quiet awakening was not shame. It was a whisper.

All my love,
Daddy

What refusal have you been postponing?

DAY 84

Dear Girls,

I don't know when it started—the habit of nodding "yes" while something in me quietly shakes its head. But I do know this: Every time I ignored that inner tremble, I walked a little farther away from myself.

There's a question that surfaced in the stillness this year, one I kept trying to silence with noise: *What refusal have I been postponing?* Not *What do you want?* Not *What dream are you chasing?* But *What are you still carrying that you should have laid down miles ago? What weight feels familiar enough to convince you it belongs?*

That word, refusal—it doesn't feel polite. It feels like a door slammed with intention. It feels like telling a toxic voice, "You no longer get to narrate my life." And I've been postponing a lot of those door slams.

But the one that got loudest this year? The refusal of false urgency. That breathless, relentless belief that everything must happen now. That if I don't respond now, I'll lose something. That if I don't achieve, post, text, reply, or deliver, someone will think less of me. The most painful part is that I started believing those things, too.

You know, I used to confuse being needed with being loved. My phone? It wasn't the addiction. It was just the dealer. The needle was approval. The high was being in control. And, the crash? The crash was what happened when silence finally caught up to me.

I remember one night, early in this year without a phone, I heard my own breath in a way I hadn't in years. Like my lungs were speaking a language I'd forgotten. And I cried—not because I was sad, but because I realized how loud my life had become. I had spent years running from the quiet, because the quiet doesn't flatter you. It doesn't applaud your productivity. It asks inconvenient questions.

It asks, "Who are you when no one needs anything from you?" And I didn't know.

So here's what I've started doing instead: I've started refusing to reply before I've thought. Refusing to feel guilty for being unavailable. Refusing to confuse efficiency with meaning. Refusing to let my worth be measured in unread messages or open tabs.

You two, you never asked for the frantic version of me. You've always just wanted my eyes. My laugh. My presence. And when

I say no to the urgency that isn't mine, when I refuse the pressure to prove or perform, I am saying yes to you.

To blueberry pancakes without a schedule.

To walks with nowhere to be.

To bedtime stories with voices and sound effects.

To Saturdays that feel like breath.

So here it is: I'm done postponing this refusal. I'm done being at the mercy of a world that rewards burnout and calls it ambition. And in case you ever find yourself caught in that same current—in case you ever feel like your value lives in how fast you answer or how much you do—I hope you hear my voice whisper back: You can say no.

You can choose slow. You can walk away from the fire everyone else is rushing into and trust that your soul was never meant to live on call. You are not a service. You are not a server. You are a miracle. Act like it.

All my love,
Daddy

What kind of prison are you living in?

DAY 89

Dear Girls,

I spent the day in prison. No, not because I did something wrong. But because I was invited to speak to a group of men who had. And if I'm being honest, I was excited. I'd been looking forward to it for weeks.

But then the drive began. And that familiar inner voice, which likes to rattle doorknobs, started whispering worst-case scenarios. What if there's a riot? What if you get stabbed? What if you get killed? You have no idea what you're walking into. It's true—the closest I'd ever been to the inside of a prison was through watching a documentary on TV.

Suddenly, this wasn't theoretical anymore. The nerves rose. The fear was real. But so was the calling, so I kept driving.

Walking in was a process, literally and emotionally. First, the metal detector. I don't remember exactly what the guard's spiel was as I was emptying my pockets, but I do remember this part: "Absolutely no cell phones allowed inside." For the first time in a long time, I chuckled. I just thought, "Well, I don't have that problem today."

It felt strange, like the first time in my life I was unintentionally following the rules just by being me. And it was a moment of unexpected lightness before the doors started locking behind me. Not one, but several. Each one closed with a loud metallic clang, a reminder that you don't get out quickly once you're in. Then I was waiting in a holding area, and then going through another door. More clanging. More nervous breathing.

Then the men walked into the chapel. Brown and blue jumpsuits. Tattoos. Some old enough to be my grandpa, some young enough to be my son.

I started shaking hands. Looking them in the eye. And it hit me: They're not much different than me. The only difference is that they got caught. I've made plenty of decisions I'm not proud of. I've gotten behind the wheel after too many drinks. Sped home on dark highways with arrogance and adrenaline. By nothing but God's grace, I didn't hit someone or something or end up behind bars.

So no, I didn't walk in there to save anyone. I walked in there to stand with them.

When it was time to speak, I wanted them to relax, so I opened with this: "We've got more in common than you think. For example, I'm currently going a full year without a cell phone...so, in some ways, I guess we're all off the grid. That is unless someone here has a phone, in which case, now would not be the time to confess. I don't want anyone to end up solitary because of me."

Laughter. And then stillness. And into that stillness, I offered the heart of my message:

"What you did is not who you are. What you wear is not your identity. God, not your past, gets the final word on your worth."

I told them about officiating. About hiding my identity behind a striped shirt and a role that made me feel important. "Some of you wear jumpsuits. I wore a whistle. But neither of those say who we are. We are more than our mistakes. We are more than our uniforms. We are the image of something holy." And something in that room shifted. I saw it. In their eyes. In their posture. Something cracked open.

Afterward, the questions came. Some of the most thoughtful questions I've ever been asked after speaking. No pretense. No posturing. Just real, raw humanity reaching for grace.

On the ride home, I couldn't stop thinking about freedom. How many of us walk around outside those gates but live like we're still locked up. Prisoners of shame. Of fear. Of regret. Trapped in stories that say you'll never change, you'll never matter, you'll never be enough.

I've lived in prisons, too. Not ones with bars or guards, but with expectations I built myself. The prison of needing to be the strong one. The wise one. The calm one. The one who has it all figured out.

I thought if I could hold everyone else up, no one would notice I was breaking. I didn't need a sentence handed down; I sentenced myself. To silence. To smiles that weren't real. To pretending I wasn't tired, or lonely, or afraid. I stayed there for years, girls—not because I couldn't leave, but because I thought staying made me good. I confused exhaustion with devotion. But there's nothing holy about abandoning yourself.

And I thought about you two. And what I want you to know, more than anything: Freedom doesn't begin when the doors open. It begins when you believe you are worthy of it—not because of what you've done, but because of who you are. And that's not up for debate. Not by the world. Not by a court. Not even by your own inner critic. It's already been decided.

You are loved.

You are seen.

You are free.

All my love,
Daddy

What would happen if we stopped bluffing?

DAY 91

Dear Girls,

There's something I need to confess.

For most of my life, I played a game I didn't even realize I was in. A high-stakes one. The kind where no one says the rules out loud, but everyone knows them: Keep your cards close. Don't show too much. Wear sunglasses. Keep a straight face. Never let people know how much you're actually feeling.

It was like I was sitting at the World Series of Poker, only the chips on the table weren't just money; they were approval, control, and belonging. My reputation. My image. My place in the world. And I played to win. But the longer I played, the more tired I became. Not just physically. But soul-tired. The kind of tiredness that sleep doesn't fix. The kind that comes from performing your life instead of living it.

I didn't know how to be seen without the costume. I didn't know how to speak without the script.

The phone was part of that. A big part. It became the perfect prop for the role I was playing. I could curate. Edit. Filter. Perform. I could respond quickly, sound smart, and look busy. I could be liked without ever having to be fully known. And when I turned the phone off, I thought the hardest part would be the disconnection. But the hardest part was the exposure. Without that little device in my hand, I couldn't hide anywhere. No screen to retreat to. No version of myself to tweak or tidy up. Just me, in the raw.

That's when clarity started showing up. It's not the kind you get from a self-help book. It's not the kind wrapped in a motivational podcast with background music and easy steps. I'm talking about the kind that creeps up in silence and whispers things you've spent years avoiding: You've been bluffing. You've been afraid. You've been lonely.

And you don't have to be anymore. There was a night, a few months in, when I sat alone at the kitchen table. Everyone else had gone to bed. No notifications. No noise. Just me, my thoughts, and the soft hum of the refrigerator. And I heard it, that ache.

That voice I'd been drowning out for years. It didn't shout. It wasn't accusatory. It just asked: Why are you still pretending?

I cried that night. Not because I was sad but because I was real. Because I wasn't trying to be anything else. No witty caption. No update to send. Just me. Unedited. And for the first time, I laid all my cards on the table. Not for anyone else, just for me.

Here's what I've come to understand, girls: Most people aren't afraid of the truth. They're afraid of what the truth demands of them. The truth doesn't just show up and sit quietly in the corner. It flips the lights on. It shatters the illusion. It forces accountability. It obliterates excuses.

Truth kills delusion. Truth kills denial. Truth kills the stories we tell ourselves to avoid change. Because once you know, you can't unknow. If you see the truth—that you're in a toxic relationship, a dead-end job, a hollow lifestyle—then you've got a decision to make.

That's what scares people. Not the truth itself. But the cost of acknowledging it. Because truth also threatens your identity. It messes with who you think you are.

If you admit you've been living small, playing it safe, hiding behind people-pleasing, then you've got to mourn the life you could have had. You've got to build a new one. That's scary if you don't have the inner scaffolding to rebuild. And let's be honest: Truth also threatens your belonging. If you stop bluffing, some people might walk away. If you tell the truth out loud, it might cost you comfort, community, or being liked.

Girls, let me tell you something I've learned the hard way: Any belonging that requires a lie isn't belonging. It's hostage-taking.

So now, I'm not bluffing anymore. Not in my work. Not in my friendships. Not in my faith. Not even with myself. Because clarity isn't always comfortable. Sometimes, it shows you things you'd rather not see—your pride, your fear, and your need to be needed.

But it's *yours. It* belongs to *you.* When you finally stop bluffing and lay it all out and say, "This is who I really am," the world may not applaud—but your soul will exhale. That's worth more than any winning hand.

All my love,
Daddy

Why don't you have your phone?

(DAY 92)

Dear Girls,

The other day, Giuliana and I had a daddy-daughter day. Just the two of us. No timeline. No agenda. No phone.

You didn't understand it yet, but you knew something was missing. "Daddy, why don't you have your phone?"

I smiled.

You wanted to listen to music in the car. And usually, I would've reached for my phone and queued up a playlist and let you pick the song. Probably Taylor Swift or the *Frozen* soundtrack.

But that day, we didn't need the music. We had your voice. We had the sound of your little boots swinging from the car seat, your stories tumbling out of your mouth faster than I could keep up.

We had the quiet hum of a fall afternoon stretched wide open for just us. You didn't know it, but you gave me something that day. You gave me presence.

We went to the library. We got lunch. We walked the Butler campus like old friends exploring a new city. And then, your first college basketball game. You danced with the mascot. You petted the bulldog. You jumped with the cheerleaders. You cheered from your seat like it was the Final Four.

And there were so many moments I would've pulled out my phone to capture. So many pictures I wanted to take, so many videos I would've recorded. Not because I wasn't present, but because I didn't want to forget.

But without knowing it, you kept pulling me back into the now. "Daddy, look!" "Daddy, did you see that?" "Daddy, I don't want to leave."

I would've left at halftime. I figured you'd be tired. I assumed the snacks would wear off and the noise would overwhelm you. But you? You stayed locked in the whole game. You didn't want to leave. You were all in. And so was I.

There were no texts to answer. No emails to check. No photos to frame. Just one girl and her dad. One afternoon, when nothing was missing.

Giuliana, you gave me the greatest gift that day. You gave me your presence. Which reminded me to give you mine. That's the kind of memory I won't need a camera for. It's the kind that prints itself on the heart.

So when you ask again, someday: "Daddy, why don't you have your phone?" I hope I remember to say: Because being with you is the only thing worth holding onto.

All my love,
Daddy

What if you're not lost, just covered up?

(DAY 95)

Dear Girls,

There's nothing quite like wearing someone else's life. Like putting on a jacket two sizes too small, smiling, and pretending you're not suffocating.

This chapter might make you uncomfortable. It made me uncomfortable to write. That's usually how I know I'm telling the truth.

Let's get something straight right out of the gate: I'm not special because I got good grades. Or made people laugh. Or crushed the sixth grade magazine fundraiser. Or because I reffed Olympic athletes. Or stood on a stage.

And I'm definitely not special because of the applause I got from peers for my success on the basketball court.

I'm special because I was created in the image of God. And so were you. That's not exclusive. That's not a trophy. It's the truth.

And it was true before I ever proved a thing. But here's where I got it wrong: I thought greatness was something I had to chase. Now, I know it's something I have to uncover. You don't get credit for potential. There's no award for hiding. You don't earn extra grace points for playing small.

The refusal to step into your personal greatness? The ducking out of your calling because you're scared, or tired, or unsure how you'll be received? That's not humility. That's avoidance.

And if I'm being real? That's an insult to God. So...sorry for insulting You, God.

We live in a world obsessed with comparison. But the only healthy comparison I've found is me versus yesterday. What did I believe yesterday? What lie did I agree with? What did I tolerate? And what one thing can I do differently today? Not five. Not ten. One.

We talk about life like it's some soul-searching journey. But I don't know if that's the right word. "Searching" implies it's lost. Like you dropped your purpose somewhere between middle school and your first heartbreak.

But maybe it's not lost. Maybe it's just covered by the noise of other people's opinions. By self-limiting beliefs you inherited but never asked for. By coping mechanisms that once helped you survive but now keep you from living.

I covered myself with performance. With likability. With hustle. I told people I was fine when I was lonely. I made people laugh so they wouldn't ask deeper questions. I wore masks for so long, I forgot what my real face looked like.

You might do it one day, too. Put on what someone else said "looked good on you." Dress up in the words "too sensitive" or "too much" or "not enough" and call it identity. But here's your permission slip (or maybe your receipt). Return those beliefs to the original sender. They don't fit you anymore.

Good news: You can uncover your truest self. Bad news: No one else can do it for you. Not your spouse. Not your pastor. Not your friends. Not even your dad. The work is yours.

Here's the line that landed in my spirit this morning: Change internal perception, then see external reflection. That's the map. Not hustle. Not pretending. Not performative self-improvement. Just small, honest work: Change the lens you're looking through. Speak better words to yourself. Refuse to tolerate what makes you shrink. Say no to what steals your light.

I've spent years going through the motions, grabbing whatever identity was easiest, living out of alignment, and yes, insulting God in the process. But I don't want to do that anymore. And I don't want that for you, either. Don't spend your life avoiding your greatness. Don't apologize for your gift. Don't bury the treasure God planted in you just because someone once told you it made them uncomfortable.

You are not too much. You are not broken. You are not lost.

You are exactly enough...when you stop covering yourself with what was never yours to carry.

Take one small step today. One shift. One choice. One returned belief. Uncover what God already knows is in you. I'm doing the same.

All my love,
Daddy

Who were you before the world told you to be someone else?

DAY 100

Dear Girls,

I used to know who I was. Before report cards. Before job titles. Before applause. I used to dream in colors the world hadn't named yet. I used to speak without rehearsing. I used to show up without wondering who I had to be.

But somewhere along the way, I traded all that in. Not just in the ordinary way children grow up. For me, officiating turned performance into a matter of survival. The whistle gave me protection—the illusion that if I called things perfectly, no one could question me, no one could hurt me. Aiming for perfection on the court bled into every corner of my life. I stopped showing up as myself and started showing up as a performance. Safe. Polished. Untouchable.

I'm not perfect. I've made mistakes. I've said the wrong thing. Stayed quiet when I should've spoken. Hurt people I love. Let fear hold the pen when faith wanted to write.

But the biggest mistake? It's abandoning the person you were born to become. It's silencing the voice inside you because the world is too loud. It's forgetting the dream you used to whisper before the world told you to grow up.

Here's the part I don't always like to admit: I got really good at appearing whole while slowly drifting away from myself.

You girls know I used to be a college basketball official. I wore the striped shirt, ran the baseline, and made the calls.

What you may not fully know, at least not yet, is how much of my identity lived inside that world. Officiating was never just a job or a hobby or a dream. It was a persona. A performance. A polished way to prove I had value.

Because that's what referees do. We control the chaos. We stay composed. We never lose our cool. We call fouls on others so no one sees the ones we commit.

We blow the whistle before anyone can get too close. But life isn't neutral. Life doesn't follow rules. And girls, life is messy.

Here's what I didn't want you to know: that I was hiding in plain sight. Not because I was ashamed. But because I forgot what it felt like to show up without the uniform. Without the mask. Without the script.

Halloween isn't the only day we wear costumes. I wore one for years.

And then the phone went away. And with it, the noise. The updates. The likes. The distraction of being seen without being known. For the first time in a long time, I had to meet myself again.

Girls, don't wait for the silence to remind you who you are. Don't wait for a breakdown to take off the mask. You are not what you do. You are not your role. You are not your résumé. You are not the version of you that makes everyone else comfortable.

You are you. And your soul remembers.

My prayer is that you never forget your name. That you never let the world rewrite it. You should never trade your voice for other people's approval. And when life tries to layer you with expectations and edits and "shoulds," you remember to return home to the truth.

Ask yourself: Who were you before the world told you to be someone else?

Because that version of you? She's still in there. She's still waiting. And she remembers.

All my love,
Daddy

What if this is all they remember?

$$\boxed{\text{DAY 107}}$$

Dear Girls,

My only rule heading into the year was that I was not going to write a book about productivity. It was my belief that the world didn't need another "how to" book on productivity or hacking your calendar. I didn't care about helping people "get more done." I cared about what we were becoming while doing all these things.

So, I did the only thing I knew how to do. I lived. I loved. I worked. I showed up. And I wrote. Every day for the first several months, I wrote without knowing where it was going. I didn't have a structure. I didn't have a publisher waiting. I didn't even know if this would turn into a book. I just kept showing up at my keyboard and telling the truth. Even when it came out messy. Even when it didn't make sense yet. Even when it scared me.

Somewhere around the halfway point, something shifted. This wasn't just a journal; it was a conversation. This was me trying to leave a light on for you. I looked over at my desk, and sitting there was the last photo I took before I turned off my phone. It was the two of you. Barefoot on a porch. Holding hands. Smiling like summer was something you were made of. And something inside me said: *That. That's why.*

From that moment on, every time I sat down to write, I looked at that photo like it was the face of my why. It felt like you'd both pulled up chairs beside me, your elbows on the table, your eyes wide and waiting. "Tell us, Daddy. What did you see today?"

And I did. I told you. I wrote like I was writing to you, because I was. I told you what I was noticing. What I was grieving. What I was learning to let go of. I told you what I wish someone had said to me when I was little. And the things I still need someone to say to me now. I didn't write these letters to sound wise.

I wrote them to stay close, to leave a trail of breadcrumbs for you to follow back to my heart, in case one day you also feel lost in this world. I told the truth while I still had the breath to say it. Because what started as a cute little experiment became a kind of resurrection. A doorway back to the things I forgot I loved.

This isn't just a book. It's a bottle I'm tossing into the ocean of your future. A legacy made of letters and longing. A way for you to know me, not just as your dad, but as a man who broke sometimes and still kept showing up. Who doubted the world, and himself, but never doubted his love for you.

Maybe, years from now, if you ever wonder what was going through your dad's heart during that strange year when he turned off his phone, you'll pull this book off the shelf, flip to any page, and feel me right there beside you. Not as a voice from the past, but as your biggest fan. Your loving father. And the guy who couldn't believe how lucky he was to call you his.

All my love,
Daddy

What if love just needs to be stirred?

DAY 110

Dear Girls,

It was a Saturday afternoon, and you both asked for peanut butter and jelly for lunch.

Simple request. We've done it a hundred times. I walked into the pantry and pulled out the jar of natural peanut butter with only two ingredients: peanuts and salt. And just as I was twisting off the lid, one of you looked up, scrunched your face, and said, "Eww. What is that?" You were pointing at the jar like it had turned into something gross. Something ruined.

But it hadn't gone bad. It had just been left alone for too long. It sat there quietly on the shelf, separating.

And later, when you were both upstairs napping, I couldn't stop thinking about that jar. Because it wasn't just peanut butter anymore. It was a metaphor for love.

Most people think love is what happens when you find the right person. But that's only

the beginning. Love, real love, the kind that lasts, is alive. And anything alive needs tending.

Let me put it like this: Love is like that jar of natural peanut butter you bought while trying to be healthier. At first, everything's together, smooth, and makes sense. But if you leave it alone and let it sit too long, it separates. The oil rises to the top, and the good stuff sinks down low.

That's what happens in relationships, too. We stop stirring. We stop reaching. We stop choosing each other in the little ways that matter.

That happened with me and your mom this year, too. Without the phone, without the constant distractions, I started to notice how easy it had become to coexist without truly connecting. We were still showing up, managing life, and loving each other... but somewhere along the way, we stopped stirring. Not out of neglect. Not out of apathy. But because life has a way of filling your hands with everything except each other.

There were nights when the house was quiet, and our silence felt louder than ever. It wasn't because anything was wrong, but because we'd gone too long without reaching. Too long without checking the jar. We hadn't lost the love. It had just settled. To be honest, there wasn't some big resolution during the year. No dramatic moment of clarity. No breakthrough scene with soft music playing in the background. But I saw it. I *finally* saw it.

Sometimes, the only way something changes is when you notice it. Because you can't stir what you won't admit has separated. What once felt easy, connected, and effortless starts to feel foreign. But that doesn't mean it's broken. It just means it's separated. And separation is natural.

So is coming back together—if you're willing to stir again. Even the best things separate when ignored. Stir it. Feel it again. Don't throw it away because you forgot how to reach for it. Closeness isn't a default setting; it's a daily decision.

You don't lose people all at once. You lose them in the pause. In the silence. In the assumption that they'll stay mixed without your help. When you feel distance creeping in, when your connection feels too thick, too sticky, too hard to spread, flip the jar. Stir it slowly. Bring everything back to the center.

Because girls, love will always ask for effort. The question is: Are you still reaching for the spoon?

All my love,
Daddy

What if love doesn't always feel like support?

DAY 116

Dear Girls,

When I decided to go a year without my phone, not everyone thought it was a good idea.

Some thought it was impractical. Some called it extreme. But the hardest reaction didn't come from strangers. It came from home.

Your mom didn't support the idea. She didn't understand why I needed to do this. And honestly, I didn't fully understand it, either; I only knew that I had to do it. There was something inside me I couldn't quiet anymore. Something calling me deeper.

But I also know this: Your mom was scared. Stressed. Tired. Carrying more than I could see. She was already holding so much weight on her shoulders, both physically and emotionally.

And my silence, my disconnection, felt like one more thing she couldn't count on.

There was a night…I can't remember what sparked it, but I remember the look. It was before my first work trip since the journey began. I was packing my bag for the trip, and walking into something exciting and important. The sun was setting. You girls were in your own swirl of chaos and joy. And your mom looked at me like I had taken something from her. Not in anger. Not in accusation. Just…weary. A look that said: "I'm holding the whole damn house together, and you get to go off chasing presence."

And here's the hardest part to admit: She wasn't wrong. But she wasn't right, either.

We were both carrying things the other didn't understand. I was carrying this ache to come back to myself. She was carrying the fear of what that might cost.

Beneath all of it, I think she worried I was growing and leaving her behind. That crushed me. Because what I couldn't seem to say clearly enough was this: I'll never apologize for growing. I believe in it too much. I needed it too much.

Now I know that I should have brought her along. Even when she didn't understand. Even when she couldn't support it. Even when the road felt like mine alone. I could've done a better job saying, "This isn't me leaving. It's me *becoming*. And I want you to be a part of that, even if we don't see it the same way yet."

It's not enough to grow quietly and hope others catch up. Love means reaching back. Even while you're moving forward. I wasn't doing this to escape. I was doing this to become. To become a better father. To become a better husband. I wanted to become the kind of man God was shaping me into.

The truth is, growth can feel like distance, especially when it happens in silence.

I told her early on, "Even if you don't understand what I'm doing, it would mean the world to feel your support."

Sometimes, as an entrepreneur, a husband, a human being, I have wild, soul-stretching ideas. I don't always need everyone to get it. But I do need someone to stand beside me and say, "I don't fully understand, but I'm with you."

I didn't get that this time. And it was the loneliest part of the journey.

But here's the part I need you to carry with you: *Just because someone doesn't understand your calling doesn't mean they don't love you. And just because someone isn't standing beside you doesn't mean they're standing against you.*

Your mom wasn't wrong for being overwhelmed. And I wasn't wrong for needing to grow. We were both right. And we were both hurting.

Sometimes, love is a long hallway. You can't see each other clearly, but you walk forward anyway. You keep showing up. Even when it's hard. Even when it's quiet. Even when it feels like you're on an island. You say yes with compassion, not defiance. You trust the growth. And you give each other room to come back.

If you ever find yourselves in a season like that, where one of you is changing and the other doesn't yet understand, don't panic. Stay gentle. Keep the door open. Speak your truth with love. And trust that real love can hold the tension between who you were and who you're becoming.

All my love,
Daddy

What if distraction is just avoidance in disguise?

Dear Girls,

Do you know what scared me the most when I first turned off my phone? It wasn't missing a call or being unreachable in an emergency, or losing out on work, or forgetting an appointment.

The scariest part was the silence. Not the quiet of the room. The quiet of me. When the buzzes and beeps died down, when there was no one I could pretend to text, no feed to scroll, no notification to chase, what I was left with was myself. That was the part I'd been avoiding.

See, the phone doesn't just keep us connected. It keeps us distracted. From the ache. From the questions we don't want to ask. From the answers we're not sure we're ready to hear.

Without the phone, I started to feel everything I had buried under years of convenience. Old memories I hadn't made peace with. Conversations I wish I'd had. Things I said too sharply. Things I didn't say when I should've. Moments I missed while I was too busy trying to capture them.

It all came rushing back in the silence. At first, I wanted to run. That's when I realized: Most of us aren't addicted to our phones. We're addicted to avoiding ourselves. Distraction feels like protection, but it's really just delay. And delay has a way of becoming a lifestyle.

We say we're "just checking," but sometimes we're really hiding. Sometimes, it's not the person across the table we're avoiding. It's the parts of ourselves we're not ready to sit with. We check our phones because we want to feel connected. But the phone can't give us what we're actually starving for.

We don't want more updates. We want to be understood. We don't want faster replies. We want deeper conversations. We don't want more content. We want more connection.

Real connection doesn't come with Wi-Fi. It comes with presence. And presence is expensive. It costs us our attention. It costs us our control. It costs us the comfort of staying half-in, just in case.

Someday, you'll sit across from someone you care about. In that moment, the most generous, most radical thing you can do is stay there. Stay in the awkwardness. Stay in the silence. Stay in the discomfort long enough to break through it. In that discomfort there is truth, healing, and real connection. The kind that doesn't just touch your screen but actually touches your soul.

So when you feel the pull to check your phone, pause. Ask yourself: What am I avoiding? And if you're brave enough, stay. Stay with the discomfort long enough to learn something from it. I promise it has something to teach you.

Distraction will always be easier, but connection will always be worth it.

All my love,
Daddy

What are we afraid will happen if we stop?

Dear Girls,

Every morning, I write. It started as a discipline. A way to document the journey. A way to keep myself accountable. But somewhere between the pen and the page, it became something more. A mirror. A flashlight. A kind of therapy that costs nothing but time and honesty.

In the silence of those early mornings, with the sun barely stretching its arms above the horizon, I find myself wrestling with questions I never made time for. Questions I didn't know I was carrying. Questions I'd been too distracted or too afraid to ask. And I think I know why most people don't write. Or sit still. Or walk without earbuds. Or leave space in the margins of their day. Because we're afraid of what will rise to the surface if we stop.

We've convinced ourselves we're too busy. That the emails

won't wait. That rest is earned. But deep down, I think we know that staying busy is just a socially acceptable way to run from ourselves.

Because when you stop, really stop, you might hear something. You might hear regret whispering from the corners of a memory you haven't visited in years. You might hear a dream you abandoned because someone once laughed at it, and it's safer to pretend it never mattered. You might hear the sound of grief knocking, soft but persistent, asking to be let in.

Or worse, you might hear nothing at all and realize you've forgotten the sound of your own voice. That was one of the hardest parts for me: realizing how long it had been since I sat with my own thoughts without trying to fix, filter, or silence them.

I wasn't just addicted to my phone. I was addicted to escape. I was addicted to noise. I was addicted to always moving.

Here's the truth: If you don't stop, you won't heal. You won't grow. You'll just loop. Like a song stuck on repeat. Familiar, but unsatisfying.

Writing every morning forced me to stop. And in that pause, I started hearing God more clearly. I believe God is always talking, but we have so many modern distractions to get us through the day that we aren't always able to hear Him. I started seeing myself without the filter of productivity or praise. I started remembering what it's like to feel. Sometimes I'd cry without knowing why. Sometimes I'd laugh out loud at something I remembered. Sometimes I'd sit in silence, unsure whether anything I was thinking made sense but trusting that showing up was enough.

If you ever feel yourself racing forward, breath caught in your chest, heart beating out of rhythm with your soul—stop. Ask yourself: What am I afraid will happen if I stop?

Maybe, just maybe, the thing you're running from is the very thing that's been waiting to heal you.

All my love,
Daddy

What if no one knows where I am?

(DAY 134)

Dear Girls,

This strange moment happens when you turn off your phone and realize that no one knows where you are. Not your family. Not your friends. Not the people who expect you to reply in five minutes or feel slighted if you don't respond in ten.

It's quiet at first. Then it's loud. Not in sound, but in questions:

Who am I...

when no one can reach me?

Who am I...

when I'm not managing someone else's expectations?

Who am I...

without a stream of text bubbles, missed calls, calendar alerts, and thumbs-up reactions?

For so long, I was tethered to obligation, approval, and the idea that being reachable made me responsible. But what if reachability and responsibility aren't the same thing?

What if always being *on* isn't a badge of honor, but a leash?

On day one, it felt like I'd amputated something vital. My pocket buzzed in ghost rhythms. I kept reaching for a phantom limb that wasn't there. But over time, the buzzing stopped. And something else began to rise beneath the silence. Me. Not the version people DM or tag in photos. Not the one who replies quickly to prove he's thoughtful. Not the one who curates a caption to sound inspiring but not *too* preachy. Just...me. The me who daydreams while walking. The me who cries while reading. The me who laughs too loudly in public, with no one to text about it.

It's wild how much of who we *think* we are is what other people reflect back to us. We rely on mirrors to name us, but some of those mirrors are warped. And if you're not careful, you'll start mistaking your reflection for your identity. You'll get so good at managing your image that you'll forget how to live from your soul.

Unplugging for a year wasn't just a detox. It was a declaration that I don't need to be constantly seen to be real. That I'm not only worth loving when I'm convenient. That solitude is not the same as loneliness.

I won't lie to you. There were days when peace felt like punishment. I missed the dopamine. I missed the distraction. I missed the illusion that I mattered because someone just texted me. There were moments when I felt forgotten. Every time I got in the car alone, I felt it again. On one hand, no one in the world could reach me. That was liberating. I could drive for hours with no destination in mind. Just me and the open road, like the steering wheel was the only thing that I remembered existed.

On the other hand, I couldn't reach anyone. And that was terrifying. That's when the voice would whisper: *They've moved on without you.* But that voice? It's just the ghost of my old life, still knocking on a locked door. Because in that emptiness, I found something my phone could never give me: peace. And in that peace, I found the depth to explore what it means to be *present*—not performing, but truly *here*.

If you ever find yourself tempted to measure your worth by how often your phone lights up, don't. Try disappearing for a little while. Not because you don't matter, but because you do. And the right people, the ones who love you, do exist even when the screen goes black. They'll still be there when you return.

All my love,
Daddy

Who am I without the whistle?

Dear Girls,

Some dreams will get under your skin so deeply that they'll feel like part of your breathing. They'll wake you up early and keep you up late. They'll stretch across years and cities, heartbreaks and tiny victories.

Sometimes, the world will clap for you. Sometimes, it will ignore you completely. Both are dangerous if you let them decide whether you keep going.

The dreams worth having, the ones that set your soul on fire, will ask you to risk disappointment, to keep showing up even when your hands are trembling. You might spend a lot of nights standing outside the place you long to be, feeling like you're not old enough, smart enough, or connected enough to walk through the door. Keep standing there, anyway. Keep listening. Keep believing.

Some dreams will hurt. They will leave marks. They will pull you through places you didn't ask to go to. But you'll find your way if you listen closely and trust the quiet music playing inside you. You'll learn that sometimes, broken hearts are just signs of a heart brave enough to have tried.

So don't be afraid to dream big often, even if it costs you. Because the only thing sadder than a broken dream is a dream that was never chased.

Officiating was that dream for me. It wasn't just a job. It wasn't even a career. It was part of my identity, etched into my bones as a teenager. Anyone who knew me then could have told you that Tommy Short would be a referee. It was a fact as sure as sunrise.

I imagined myself calling games deep into my sixties and seventies, silver-haired, maybe a little slower getting up and down the court, but still there, still needed, still mattering. Then, one day, I wasn't. I left officiating after nearly two decades, not because I stopped loving it, but because I knew that deep in my soul something else was calling me.

I couldn't name it yet. Speaking wasn't even on the radar. Writing a book back then would have been laughable. I didn't have a business plan, a platform, or a roadmap. All I had was a stirring. A restlessness that wouldn't leave me alone. A whisper that said, *You were made for more.* Not more in the flashy, ego-driven sense. Not more followers, more applause, more accolades. More soul. More surrender. More truth.

Leaving officiating was the most terrifying thing I had ever done. Because I wasn't just leaving a career. I was leaving an identity. I was stepping away from the one thing I knew how to be. The thing other people respected me for, the thing that gave structure and meaning to my days.

And the fear that rose up wasn't about money or failure. It was a quieter, more devastating fear: Do I still matter without the whistle?

Because here's what I've learned about chasing dreams: If it doesn't scare you, it probably isn't worth doing. And the thing that scares me most isn't rejection, or starting over. It's living a life without meaning. Waking up ten years from now, realizing I never asked deeper questions. That I kept doing what I was good at, long after it stopped making me whole. That I never risked the wilderness long enough to find out who I really was.

For two years after I left, I couldn't go near a college basketball court. I couldn't walk into an arena. I couldn't even bear to watch a game on TV. Not because I was bitter or didn't love the game anymore. But because every squeak of sneakers on hardwood, every whistle blast, and every roar of the crowd echoed inside the hollow space where my identity used to live. I didn't know how to just be another face in the stands. I didn't know how to sit still without the uniform, role, or certainty that I belonged.

There were days I almost turned the phone back on. There were days I almost tried to run back into officiating to resurrect the life I had laid down. Because belonging is addictive, too. Because certainty feels like oxygen when you're gasping for air.

But I didn't go back. I stayed in the ache. I stayed in the silence.

I endured the slow, brutal process of remembering who I was without the whistle.

And what I learned, slowly, painfully, is that I matter because I am. Not because I produce. Not because I perform. Not because I win applause. But because I exist. Because I am loved by a God who saw me before the first whistle blew and will love me long after the final buzzer sounds.

The dream of officiating was beautiful. It shaped me into who I am today. It strengthened me and taught me about discipline, integrity, and courage. But it wasn't my whole name. It wasn't my whole soul.

Maybe that's the hidden mercy of broken dreams: They bring us back to ourselves. Not the polished, impressive selves we project to the world, but the *real* selves. The ones who are still worthy, still loved, even when nobody's clapping.

If you're standing outside the life you used to know, if you're staring at a closed door and wondering who you are without the title, the uniform, the old dream stay. Stay long enough to hear the deeper voice. Stay long enough to find out you're still breathing, burning, and beloved.

Because sometimes, losing everything you thought you needed is the only way to discover who you are.

All my love,
Daddy

Why are we always in such a hurry?

Dear Girls,

I used to believe I didn't have five minutes. I used to believe I was that important.

That all changed one evening, quietly, without any sort of ceremony.

We were driving home from the grocery store. No deep conversations, no epiphanies, just a backseat full of snacks and two kids singing out of sync. And then, without thinking, I took a right instead of a left. Just to try something new. Just to see what else was out there.

We eventually found our way home. When we pulled into the driveway, you both burst through the door like explorers returning from the edge of the world.

"We found a *new, new way home!*" you told Mom, faces lit with pride.

I didn't think much of it. Just a sweet little moment. A blip. But you remembered. Kids always remember the magic we almost miss.

The next morning, while the clock whispered its usual threats and the to-do list drummed in my brain, you both, at the exact same time, said, "Daddy, let's take the *new, new* way to school."

I almost said no. I almost let the schedule win. Because that's what grown-ups do: We sacrifice wonder at the altar of "just trying to stay on track." We pick the same roads, not because they're right, but because they're fast.

But something in me paused. Something that had gone still since putting the phone down stirred and whispered: *What if this is the point?*

So we took the new, new way. And somewhere along that detour, we passed a little park. The one we'd always said we'd stop at "sometime" but never did.

It was gray that morning. Rain threatened to write its name across the sky. And then I said something ridiculous: "What if we stopped and played at the park *before* school?"

Your eyes. God, your eyes. You looked at me like I'd just rewritten gravity. So we stopped. We played. We laughed. You climbed and swung like time had loosened its grip. The rain came soon after, and we ran for the car—soaked just enough to remember. And then we went to school. Like nothing happened. But something *did* happen. Something holy.

Since then, I keep wondering: How many "new, new ways" have I ignored because I thought I didn't have time? How many magic parks passed by in a blur of deadlines and destinations? All because I had places to be. Emails to answer. Deadlines to chase.

I told myself five minutes wasn't worth the risk of running late. That five minutes was too expensive. That five minutes wasn't *productive* enough. But after I turned off my phone, something unexpected happened. I started seeing my life from above. Not after it passed me by, but *right in the middle of it.* Hindsight, live and in color.

I saw how your eyes lit up when I said yes. Heard your laughter echo off the car windows like bells. Felt how five minutes stretched out like a lifetime, folded inside an ordinary Tuesday. And I felt the sting, too. The slump in your shoulders when I said no. The silence that settled in the car. The way I checked an invisible watch like the world would crumble if I was late to it.

Was I saving time? Or just *spending it badly*?

Before the sky opened that morning at the park, you didn't ask for much. You didn't need a grand adventure. You just needed me to say yes.

We had maybe five minutes. Five minutes of wet slides and squeals. Of swinging so high the ground blurred. Of stories about clouds and feet splashing in mud. Five minutes that ended with soaked hair, full hearts, and me carrying you back to the car like treasure.

Later that same night, after dinner, when the rain returned, we didn't hide from it. We ran straight into it. Through the backyard, then the front. Your feet slapping puddles, your hands catching raindrops like secrets. You called it a "worm adventure." You knelt down in the mud to rescue earthworms inching across the sidewalk. You didn't mind the mess. You didn't mind the rain. You only minded if we missed it.

Girls, I used to believe I didn't have five minutes. But the truth is: I didn't have five minutes to waste.

And now? Now, I'm not waiting for five minutes to magically appear. I'm choosing them. I'm *stacking* them. Like bricks in a home we're building together. Five minutes to sit longer at breakfast. To linger at the door when you wave goodbye. To ask one more question at bedtime. To say yes to the park, the puddles, the worms, the wonder. Because five minutes here, five minutes there, they grow. Into hours. Into days. Into the stories we'll tell when you're grown, and I'm just a man at the edge of memory, grateful for every moment I didn't rush through.

Here's what no one says loud enough: *You don't just make memories. You choose them.* Five minutes at a time.

So here's my promise: When the choice is between hurrying and holding on, between getting there faster or seeing you clearer...I'll choose you. Every time.

All my love,
Daddy

What if the airport was a time machine?

DAY 149

Dear Girls,

I walked into the airport with a stack of papers so thick I half expected TSA to hand me a binder clip and say, "Godspeed."

Boarding pass. Hotel confirmation. Rental car reservation. Driving directions. A printed agenda for the conference I was attending. It looked less like a business trip and more like I was preparing for a trial.

But there I was. No phone. No app to tell me if my gate had changed. No text alert if my flight was delayed. Just me and a row of blinking monitors that might as well have been hieroglyphics. I used to mock the people who stood under those big airport monitors, squinting up because the font is always six sizes too small. I'd smirk and think, *Just check your phone like a normal person.*

After landing, I didn't select the GPS option for the rental car. I was feeling bold. Some people chase adrenaline with skydiving. I chased mine with a glove box of printed-out driving directions folded like treasure maps. Marked them up with highlighters like I was studying for a final exam in *How Not to Get Lost in a City You've Never Been To*. And for a few brief, hilarious moments, I was seventeen again. Speeding up the hill toward Cathedral High School in my '93 gold Mercury Sable, driver's seat irresponsibly reclined, a cherry-scented air freshener swinging like a metronome for my bad decisions, while nineties hip-hop made my speakers rattle like they had asthma.

Back then, I thought MapQuest was high-tech. I thought burning a mix CD was an act of love. And I thought I had all the time in the world. Now, at forty-one, I sit up straighter when I drive. I listen to podcasts about emotional intelligence. And I find myself romanticizing wrong turns because they remind me I'm still learning.

The funniest part of this whole trip? I didn't die. I didn't need my phone to keep me safe or sane. I just needed a little patience. A little paper. A little courage to look up.

Maybe that's what this whole year has been about. Realizing that the modern world makes you think you *can't* do anything without a phone. But when you strip it all away, you don't lose your ability to function. You just lose your excuse to stop paying attention.

Girls, the first time I flew without a phone wasn't a burden. It was a gift. A reminder that adventure isn't about knowing exactly where you're going. It's about getting a little lost on purpose. And trusting that you'll figure it out.

All my love,
Daddy

What if you didn't need permission?

(DAY 154)

Dear Girls,

Too often in life, we don't chase a big vision of the future because of the small, boring inconveniences in the present. We trade extraordinary tomorrows for comfortable todays. We shrink dreams down until they fit inside calendars and to-do lists. We call it being "realistic," but really, it's just forgetting who we are.

If I could leave you with one thing, one gift, one blueprint, one whispered secret to carry through your whole life, it would be this: You'll never need anyone else's permission to live a life you're proud of. *Ever*.

You already have it. Because in our house, there's only one word you're not allowed to say: can't. If I hear it slip from your mouth, I'll come running from the other room like the place is on fire. Not because I'm mad, but because I refuse to let that word plant itself in your mind. I don't care if it's tying your shoes or opening a snack—"can't" has no place here. I want you to grow up believing, in your bones, that you are capable. That no obstacle is too big, no dream too out of reach.

And maybe right now it feels a little silly, maybe you roll your eyes when I correct you after hearing "can't." But one day, when you're standing face-to-face with something hard, and you hear a quiet voice inside, I hope it says, "I can do this." You'll realize that what I was really doing all along was building your self-belief, one small moment at a time.

This year, I gave myself a permission slip no one else could write for me. I said yes to something that made no sense on paper. I said yes to the long way around.

I risked being laughed at. I risked being invisible. I risked being misunderstood.

I would do it all again. Because nothing unforgettable ever starts with safety. It starts with a whisper. It starts with a reckless kind of hope. It starts when you choose to believe that even if the world never claps, God still smiles.

The truth is, the world will try to invoice you for your courage. They'll call you reckless when you dream too loud. They'll say you're naïve when you trust your gut more than their blueprint.

But hear me: It is not your job to make yourself smaller so they can feel comfortable. It is not your duty to bleed yourself dry just to be palatable. You are not a museum artifact meant to be admired behind glass. You are wildfire and symphony and sea surge all tied into one. You were born to disrupt.

If the dream inside you makes people uncomfortable? Good. It means you're doing it right. It means you're shaking the foundations of a world that forgot how to be brave. It means you are alive in the way that most people are too scared to be.

The world might look different when you are old enough to read this. Brighter in some ways. Louder in others. But there's something the future will never erase: Nothing great ever comes from playing it safe.

I didn't silence my phone because it was a smart strategy. I didn't walk away from the noise because it made sense to anyone else. I did it because my soul was starving. Because something inside me was desperate for a life that wasn't curated, predicted, or controlled.

Here's the thing most people are too scared to say out loud: The best things in life, the real and lasting things, almost always look crazy at first. They start as tiny seeds the world calls foolish. Dreams too tender for public consumption. Visions too big for small minds.

Maybe this book won't sell a million copies. Maybe it won't trend or go viral or be framed in gold. But it may have already done what it was meant to do. Because maybe it set me free. Maybe it cracked something open in me that can never be shut again. Maybe it taught me that the bravest thing you can ever do is begin anyway.

Leap anyway. Believe anyway. Even if the applause never comes. Even if no one else understands. Because living a life you're proud of has never been about impressing the world. It's always been about answering the whisper calling your name.

And both of you *are* made for that kind of life. The wild one. The brave one. The one you don't need permission for. Only courage. So keep going.

Because at the end of the day, the loudest applause you'll ever hear is the sound of your soul saying, "Well done." You'll make others uncomfortable sometimes, but you should always make yourself proud.

All my love,
Daddy

What if you can hear who you're becoming before fully believing it?

DAY 160

Dear Girls,

There's a version of me I haven't fully met yet. But I can hear him. He's been whispering all year—not shouting, not demanding, just gently flicking the light down the hallway, waiting for me to walk toward him.

For most of my life, I didn't even know he existed. I was too busy curating the man everyone else expected. Too busy being liked to ask what I really believed. Too busy being needed to wonder who I was becoming.

But this year, the silence stripped away the noise. And under all the layers, I found something unexpected: My voice. Not loud. Not polished. Not selling anything. Just true.

I started to ask myself: What if this voice isn't some fantasy? What if this voice is me, becoming?

Girls, there was a shift that happened when I was officiating, one I didn't fully understand until now. I went from wanting to be liked to wanting to be respected. At first, I stepped onto the court, hoping every coach, every player, and every fan would approve of me. That they'd say I was fair, kind, humble, likable. That I could fit in.

Over time, I learned something that changed me: Not everyone will like you. But they can still respect you. And that distinction, between approval and integrity, shaped something deeper in me. Because respect is quiet. It's not about applause. It's about alignment. That's what I've been learning to listen for this year—not the noise of other people's expectations, but the internal clarity of who I'm meant to become.

Maybe years later, there's a version of me who doesn't flinch at being misunderstood. Who isn't auditioning for attention. Who doesn't need the applause to keep walking. And I want to be that man.

I've caught glimpses of him already. When I started writing, I wasn't trying to impress anyone. I didn't even think I was a writer. I just showed up. One blog post at a time.

Somewhere in that practice, I stopped caring about outcomes. I stopped writing for recognition. I started writing because something true was trying to get out. That's when I started to surprise myself—not with how "good" the writing was, but with how real it felt. How unarmored.

I want you to know this, girls: Sometimes, your future self will come to find you. Not with fireworks, but with stillness. Sometimes, the version of you waiting down the road doesn't need you to speed up. She just needs you to listen. To keep showing up. To stop playing small. To stop waiting for applause before you believe you're enough.

I still have moments when fear sneaks in and says, *What if this doesn't work? What if no one gets it? What if you're too much?* But I remind myself: Fear isn't real. It's only our imagination focused in the wrong direction.

And the man I'm becoming? He's not afraid of being too much. He's afraid of settling for less than the truth. He knows faith doesn't require a perfect plan. It requires only the courage to keep walking toward the light.

So I'm walking. I'm listening. I'm learning to love the sound of my soul finally speaking.

All my love,
Daddy

What if the mirror doesn't lie?

$$\boxed{\text{DAY 163}}$$

Dear Girls,

I've been thinking a lot about mirrors. How they don't flatter. How they don't argue. How they don't adjust to make you feel better. They just reveal.

I've come to believe that real listening, the kind that transforms you, is like looking in a mirror. Not to judge. Not to shame. Only to see.

Most of us don't really want to see. We want to edit. We want to filter. We want to hear the version of the truth that keeps us comfortable. And I'll be honest: I've done that for most of my life.

But this year? The silence didn't let me get away with it. It became the mirror I couldn't avoid. What it showed me wasn't always flattering.

There's a saying that you become the average of your five closest friends. If that's true, I'm incredibly blessed, because my five closest friends are strong men. Family men. Men who show up. Men I admire.

Here's the uncomfortable part: I don't know if I'd make their list. Not because they don't love me, but because I've wrestled with feeling "less than." Less successful. Less stable. Less financially secure.

The truth is, I've made some choices I'm not proud of, especially when planning for your future. I've made investments that didn't pan out. I've chased dreams that cost more than they paid. I've operated more from passion than from strategy.

There were moments this year when I had to ask myself: Am I building a future for my family or just chasing an image of myself? That question hurt. Because I didn't always like the answer. There were days when shame crept in—not for something I did, but for what I didn't do. For what I failed to build. For how far behind I sometimes felt. It's not that I need to be the richest dad on the block, but I want to be the kind of man who prepares. Who plans. Who provides. That's the truth the silence revealed. Not to punish me. But to wake me up.

In that honesty, I also saw something else: Maybe my friends wouldn't trade places with me. But maybe there are parts of me they admire. My faith. My vulnerability. My willingness to walk away from comfort for the sake of something deeper.

I don't know. I haven't asked them. But I do know this: Listening isn't about comparison. It's about congruence. It's about asking: Are my choices aligned with the man I want to become? Or am I still performing for applause that don't fill me?

A part of me still wants to be "the good guy." The guy who gets it right. Who doesn't let anyone down. But maybe that part of me doesn't need to be protected. Maybe he just needs to hear this: You don't need to be perfect to be good. You don't need to be wealthy to be worthy. You don't need to have it all together to raise daughters who believe they are deeply loved.

Girls, if there's one thing I hope you take from this letter, it's this: When you stand in front of your own mirror, whether it's silence, stillness, or someone who loves you enough to tell you the truth, don't flinch. Don't turn away. Even if the reflection stings, keep looking.

Because that pain? It's not shame. It's a signal. It's your soul asking to be realigned. Let it. Because the mirror doesn't lie. It just reveals. Sometimes, that's the bravest listening we'll ever do.

All my love,
Daddy

What if listening is the only inheritance I leave you?

(DAY 168)

Dear Girls,

Lately, I've been wondering: What if the inheritance I leave you isn't something you can hold or spend, but only something you grow into? What if it's not a house, a car, or even a list of stories, but a way of being? A posture? A presence?

I'm starting to believe the most sacred thing I could ever pass down to you is knowing how to listen. And not just listen the way the world does: ears half-tuned, fingers half-scrolling, eyes darting to the next notification.

I mean real listening. Whole-body listening. Full-heart listening. The kind of listening that doesn't just wait for its turn to speak but makes *room*. That doesn't just hear words but hears *longing*. That doesn't just react but *responds.* Slowly, gently, truthfully.

I have to tell you something: I didn't know how to do that until this year. Until I turned off my phone. Until the noise went quiet enough for me to notice what I'd been missing all along.

You'd be surprised what you can hear when there's no buzzing in your pocket. No screen on the table. No tether to the outside world demanding your attention. When the phone disappears, something else rises up in its place. Stillness. Curiosity. God. You.

I started hearing things I never used to notice. The way someone swallows when they're nervous. The way their shoulders shift when they're about to share something tender. The way their voice catches mid-sentence, revealing what they didn't say. I began to hear sorrow buried under silence. Hope woven into hesitation. Joy humming just beneath the surface.

And what I've found, girls, is this: When someone feels truly heard, they start to remember who they are. They come back to life. They soften. They unfold. That's what I want to give you. Not advice. Not answers. Not a roadmap. But a lantern made of presence.

Because if you can learn how to listen like this—to your friends, your partner, your God, your own soul—you'll be the rarest kind of person in the room. Not the loudest. The safest. And one day, you'll sit across from someone you love—maybe your own daughter, perhaps a stranger with tear-filled eyes—put away your phone, lean in and say, *"I'm here,"* without needing to fix anything.

That's me. That's my legacy, living on through you. Here's what

I pray you'll remember: When the world gets noisy, make space for silence. When the anxiety feels overwhelming, make space for God. When someone speaks, look them in the eye. When you feel the urge to reach for your phone, reach for their heart instead.

When you find yourself aching to feel close to me someday, long after I'm gone, maybe don't look for my words. Just listen. To the stillness. To the truth under the noise. To the love I tried to embody in how I showed up, not just what I said. Because that's where I'll be. Right there. In the way you listen.

Maybe that's why something hit me like a quiet truth dropped in my lap: *listen* and *silent* share the same letters. Rearranged but inseparable. It's almost as if the universe wanted to leave us a clue: If you want to truly listen, you need to be silent.

If you want to be silent, you need to *want* to listen. That's what I had forgotten how to do. And that's what this year provided me.

All my love,
Daddy

What are you filling the silence with?

(DAY 171)

Dear Girls,

I met a friend for breakfast a few months into this no-phone year. Nothing profound, just a hole-in-the-wall spot with strong coffee and mismatched chairs.

I arrived first, and without a phone to scroll, I started noticing. That's when it happened, like something from a National Geographic documentary. Two women, probably business associates, were sitting at the table next to me. One of them politely excused herself to use the restroom. Suddenly, the woman left behind was alone.

The shift was instant. Her eyes darted. Her posture tightened. Her hand, almost instinctively, slipped into her bag like a Navy SEAL disarming a bomb. She pulled out her phone with this practiced, stealthy motion, like if she moved too fast, the loneliness might notice. She stared at it like it would give her oxygen.

And here's the thing: I didn't judge her. Because I *recognized* her. That used to be me. I knew that itch. That reflex. That silent panic that says: *Quick, distract yourself before the quiet gets weird.*

We don't wait anymore. We *escape.* From lines. From elevators. From the person in front of us. From ourselves. And that moment at breakfast, it stuck with me. Because when you don't have a phone to look at, you start to see the world again. You become an observer. Not a participant in the dopamine arms race, but a witness to it.

And one of the most sobering things I've realized is this: *We are bored being bored. We* don't just hate silence; we've forgotten how to sit inside it. We're no longer deliberate with our dopamine. We chase it like thirst in a desert, pulling it from whatever screen, scroll, or stimulation we can get our hands on.

Boredom used to be a doorway. Now it's a fire alarm. But I'm learning: Silence isn't something to survive. It's something to *listen to.* It's not empty; it's full. Full of the stuff we've been trying to mute: the griefs we've shelved; the questions we're afraid to answer; the dreams we buried because they didn't make money; the aches we mistake for weakness.

Maybe that's the real addiction—not to the phone itself, but to the *escape* it offers when life feels too honest. We use our screens like pacifiers. Not because we're weak, but because we're human. Life is unpredictable, and we want something to hold when it all starts spinning.

But girls, hear me when I say this: Don't fear the silence. *Prac-*

tice it. Because silence doesn't just make room for the soul, it introduces you to it.

Now, when I'm in the quiet, I make tea. I light a candle. I listen to the sound the spoon makes against the side of the mug. I don't try to fill the space. I let the space fill *me.* Because I've learned this: If you can't sit in boredom, you'll never find wonder. If you can't be alone with your thoughts, you'll never know which ones are yours. And if you run every time it gets quiet, you'll miss the only voice that really matters.

I've been asking myself: *What am I filling the silence with?* And what if I left it unfilled? What would rise up? What would finally breathe? What would heal?

Girls, I know it sounds strange, but this year without a phone has taught me how to be home in myself again. Not when I've achieved something. Not when I'm needed. But right now. In the boring. In the in-between. In the five-minute wait when nothing is happening and everything still matters.

We are bored being bored. But boredom is a teacher. It points to our unhealed places. It clears space for creativity. It's where your truest voice waits to be heard.

Here's my hope for you: When the silence comes—and it *will*—don't panic. Don't reach. Don't scroll. Don't fix it. Just be. Let your soul speak. Let boredom stretch its legs. Let wonder find you without a screen to tell it where to go. Because the truth is, you don't have to fill the silence. You just have to stop running from it.

All my love,
Daddy

What if the clearance rack is where the joy is?

(DAY 174)

Dear Girls,

Some days, joy doesn't show up on schedule. It doesn't burst through the door wearing a party hat. It whispers from the back right corner of Office Depot.

That's where I found it this week, tucked behind discount pencil sharpeners and half-used notebooks: a twenty-five-pack of miniature books for five dollars. Six pages each. Four words a page. Nothing epic. Except for the way you both lit up in the backseat when I started reading them like a dramatic, shouting sports announcer: "The...BLUE...DOG...JUMPS!"

You howled. You clapped. You begged for more. And I realized something I've been slow to learn: You don't need expensive things. You need engaging things. You need me, undistracted. Present enough to make a plastic book feel like a Broadway debut. That moment didn't cost much, but it paid out more than most things ever will.

This phone-free life has taught me how to find value in the overlooked aisle.

It's made me a clearance rack kind of dad. Not because I'm cheap, but because I've learned how rich *ordinary* can be.

Joy isn't always waiting in the places we chase it. Sometimes, it's sitting quietly in the back of the store, hoping someone will notice it without needing a notification.

All my love,
Daddy

What if joy comes dressed like an interruption?

Dear Girls,

I nearly missed it.

The sacred moment didn't arrive during meditation. It didn't come from a mountaintop, a journal prompt, or a whisper in the trees. It came from a sound I hadn't heard in years: the jingle of an ice cream truck rolling through our neighborhood.

It was around 8:00 p.m., and you both were already tucked in for the night. Pajamas on. Bedtime stories read. Routine in place. That ever-so-satisfying sense of "done."

But then I heard it. That melody. That tug. That invitation. And everything in me knew: *Go.* It was such a small thing. A silly thing, really. But I'm learning that the holy things often come dressed like that: silly, spontaneous, interruptive.

I ran into your rooms and shouted, "The ice cream truck is here!" We threw on some shoes, grabbed some cash, and chased it down. Not just for the ice cream, but also for the moment it offered: both of you, your mom, sticky fingers, and chocolate smiles.

That night, I was reminded of something the silence had been trying to teach me: Presence isn't always structured. Sometimes, it comes disguised as a detour. A soft rebellion against the tyranny of discipline.

Because while I've been focused on stripping away distraction, on seeking stillness and order, I'm also learning that joy lives in the interruptions.

That ice cream, that night, with both of you giggling...it opened up something in my chest. A kind of sweet ache. A reminder of why I'm doing this at all.

This isn't just about breaking an addiction. It's about becoming more interruptible. More alive to the moment when life offers you a gift, unexpected and melting fast, and you don't let it pass you by.

It was a great reminder: Don't worship your routine so much that you forget to be human. Don't miss the music. Don't miss the memory that might outlive you.

I didn't return to bed thinking, "I crushed that day." I returned to bed thinking, "That's the kind of dad I want to be."

All my love,
Daddy

What do you hear when you finally get quiet?

(DAY 178)

Dear Girls,

I did something strange on day two of my no-phone year. I walked into a restaurant, ordered takeout, and sat down on a bench. Alone. With only a pen and paper. No phone. No email. No checking in, scrolling, responding, pretending to be busy. Just me. Just breath. Just stillness in public, a radical act these days.

At first, it felt awkward, like I was doing something wrong. Like I had accidentally broken an invisible rule about "looking normal" when you're alone. I shifted in my seat. I looked at my hands. I felt the tug, that old itch, to look busy. To prove to no one in particular that I had somewhere else to be.

But then, I breathed. And I listened. Not for someone's voice. Just for everything.

Here's what I heard: An upbeat remix of Taylor Swift, dancing on the edge of background noise, not quite loud enough to ask the manager to turn it down, but just insistent enough to remind you it's there. I couldn't Shazam the song. No phone. So instead of grabbing it, I let it reach me. And it did.

Nearby, a little girl, three or four, resisted her mother's quiet pleas to sit still. Not crying. Not scared. Just deeply committed to *not complying*. Her protest was a masterpiece.

I understood only like a parent with young children can. I've got two of you in that stage. I felt her fire in my chest like a memory. I empathized silently.

From the kitchen: the sharp clang of pans. A stack of plates clinked together with just enough force to say, *Someone back there is not having a good day.*

The AC kicked on with a low hum, followed by the soft whir of a mixer, pulsing like a heartbeat: steady, necessary, unnoticed until it wasn't. The front door creaked, an old groan that practically begged for WD-40. A hostess, probably seventeen, accidentally rang the wrong number for an order. Her eyes widened like she'd triggered a national emergency. I wanted to tell her: *You're going to be okay. This isn't the end. It's barely a blip. One day, you'll laugh about this.* But I let her sit in it. That's how we learn to breathe again.

Then, an older man, jaw clenched, barked into his speakerphone. He paced like the floor owed him something. It wasn't about the call. It was about being heard. Or maybe about being unheard for too long.

I heard all of this. Not because I was *trying* to. But because I wasn't trying *not* to. I wasn't distracted. I was present. Presence is what turns *sound* into *the story*. In just twenty-one minutes, I heard more of the world than I had in years. Because most of the time, we're not listening. We're waiting. We're preparing to speak. We're bracing for the next ping. We're half-here, half-somewhere else. We're responding instead of receiving.

That day, for the first time in a long while, I didn't listen to respond. I listened to understand. And that changed everything.

Girls, I hope you'll remember this: Silence isn't empty. It's *full* of things that are usually too quiet to compete. Love. Compassion. Insight. Truth. God.

The more I listen, the more I realize that the calls I was waiting for wouldn't come through a phone. They were already happening. I just needed to be still enough to hear them.

All my love,
Daddy

What can the middle teach you that the beginning never could?

(DAY 180)

Dear Girls,

They say you don't know how far you've come until you stop and look back. Well, I'm halfway through this journey with no phone, no maps, and no notifications telling me where to go next. Just stillness. Questions. This pen and too many notebooks to count.

At the start of the year, I thought I'd write a book about turning off my phone. I didn't know that I'd also be turning down the volume on the world, on other people's opinions, on who I thought I had to be. And when the noise faded, all that was left was the sound of my own soul clearing its throat, asking if I was finally ready to listen. I've had more questions than answers. But that's where the light started to leak in. And so, from the middle of the story, not the end, I want to share what

I'm learning. Not to preach. Not to perform. Just to say what's becoming true for me. Maybe, one day, it will speak to you too.

The first thing I've learned is this: *Things that don't matter don't matter.* Not just in theory, but in practice. Most things I used to consider urgent or critical are unimportant. What I care about has narrowed. Sharpened. Softened.

At the end of the day, I only want to have an opinion on three things: my faith, my family, and my life's work. Everything else is noise dressed up as relevance.

I've surprised myself, too. I thought I'd miss sports. The endless stats, the highlight reels. But I don't. I thought I'd crave the connection of social media. But I don't. What I've craved most is presence. Peace. Silence. And, unexpectedly, writing.

I've written more in 180 days than I had in thirty-nine years. Some of it might find a home in this book. Most of it won't. But it's healed me in places I didn't know were broken.

I also started therapy, remember? I sat in a waiting room and looked around like I was on a movie set. I kept thinking, "Now what?"

The truth? Nothing dramatic happened. I just talked. And for the first time in a long time, someone asked questions that came not with answers but with mirrors. Gentle ones, held up to help me see.

I'm learning that just because you turn away from something doesn't mean it goes away. Avoidance isn't peace. It's just procrastinated pain. I've learned that how people speak to themselves and others reveals more than they realize. I've heard "must be nice" and "I wish I could" way too often. Too much victimhood hiding inside sarcasm. I've realized I've said some of those things, too.

I felt judgment creep in while watching others scroll through their phones and scroll past their own lives. But eventually, I saw the truth; I was really judging the parts of me I didn't want to face. My own autopilot. My own discomfort with stillness. My own escape routes.

There's no hesitation when someone asks you your address; you rattle it off without thinking. That's how I want to know myself. On that level. Instinctual. Intimate. Undeniably home. We don't need more time. We need more clarity.

We live like people who open Google Maps without a destination and then wonder why we feel lost. A detour only exists when you have a direction. And maybe the road we're on was never ours to begin with.

I've lost people this year. A mentor who meant the world to me. Pain like that doesn't announce itself. It just arrives and unpacks its bags. But I've learned grief doesn't mean life stops. It means you pay more attention to what actually matters while it continues.

I've spent solo walks thinking about legacy more than anything else. Not legacy in the spotlight. Legacy in the hallway. Legacy in the bedtime routine. Legacy in how you treat a restaurant server, not how you speak on a stage.

Some friends I thought were close haven't reached out once. Others have shown up in ways I'll never forget. Growth does that. It clarifies the room.

I've learned that growth doesn't always look like movement. Sometimes, it looks like sitting still. I don't know what the second half of this journey will hold. But I do know this: *What you get isn't as important as who you become.*

Complaining is a luxury we don't have time for. Silence is not the absence of something. It's the presence of everything. If someone says, "You've changed," I'll take that as the highest compliment.

I don't have the ending yet. But I know what I'm after now. Not perfection. Not control. Just presence. Just peace. Just being the kind of man you'd be proud to call your dad.

All my love,
Daddy

What if the call doesn't come with a ringtone?

(DAY 185)

Dear Girls,

I had time between meetings the other day, so I sat outside a coffee shop and just…noticed. No agenda. No scrolling. Just stillness. People-watching. Sipping something warm.

The sun stretched across the sidewalk like it was trying to eavesdrop. The air smelled like roasted coffee beans and the tail end of someone's vanilla perfume. A couple laughed too loud behind me. Pigeons fought over crumbs like old men playing dominoes with something to prove.

And it hit me: Silence isn't the absence of sound. It's the presence of something more profound. Not an empty room, but a doorway. Not a void, but a canvas, wide and waiting, where the soul finally paints.

That's when I realized: The miracle of stillness isn't that it gives you more to say. It reveals what you've been too noisy to hear. We live in a world that runs from quiet. We've confused immediacy with importance. Information with wisdom. Connection with communion. Noise with presence.

And I used to be right there with it. Whenever someone mentioned a book or a show or a stat over coffee, I'd feel that old reflex to reach for my phone. Look it up mid-conversation, like urgency was the same thing as curiosity.

But now? If an answer isn't worth remembering by the time I get home, maybe it wasn't essential to begin with.

My value isn't in my access. It's in my attention. It's in where I point my presence. So I ask myself: Is this urgent, or just familiar? Essential, or just easy? Most of the time, the need to *know* fades before I even reach for a screen. And what I'm left with is stillness.

Not emptiness. But a sanctuary. A place where I don't just find answers; I uncover better questions. Because God doesn't compete with noise. He waits for a quiet heart.

And not all whispers are holy.

Some voices sound like comfort but feel like compromise. Some temptations speak in convenience, not truth. That's why I need the quiet. To know the difference. To hear the real *Call*. And girls, when your moment comes, when your call arrives, I hope you're brave enough to answer it. Even if it doesn't ring. Even if everything in you wants to stay busy, numb, and loud.

Take off the headphones. Let the quiet in.

All my love,
Daddy

What if every test was a gift in disguise?

(**DAY 191**)

Dear Girls,

You're learning so much in school: vowels, consonants, numbers, and shapes. You tell me, proud and wide-eyed, that the vowels are A, E, I, O, U. And I love how excited you are to share what you know.

But I have a secret. They're teaching you the right letters but not the right order. The real order, the one life will whisper when things get hard, is this: E. I. A. O. U. Everything. Is. An. Opportunity. For U.

See, school teaches you the lesson first. You study, you memorize, and *then* comes the test. But life? Life flips the script. Life tests you first. It pops the quiz before you've even opened the book.

Sometimes, it pulls the chair out from under you, and all you have left are your knees. Only then does the lesson arrive. And it won't come with gold stars or checkmarks. It'll come through heartache. Through silence. Through missed chances and the quiet ache of growing. Through laughter that saves you and losses that shape you.

Let me tell you a story.

It was the end of my final season officiating college basketball. Almost two decades. Countless flights. Thousands of nights away from home. Deep down, I knew I was done. You were just a few months old, Giuliana. I was in an elevator, late in the season, still wearing the identity I'd carried for so long. Delta Medallion tags hung on my suitcase, dangling like a trophy.

A man stepped in, saw me, and said, "Wow, you must travel all the time. That's the life, huh?"

I didn't even look up from my phone. I said, "It's not that cool. It just means I'm away from my family." In that moment, everything shifted. What once felt like a badge of honor now felt like distance. What once looked like achievement now felt like absence. What I thought gave me value now reminded me how far I was from home.

That was the sign. The quiet truth I couldn't unhear.

See, everything depends on how you choose to see it.

Whether it's a test in school, a hard season in life, or a stranger in an elevator, remember this: E. I. A. O. U. Everything. Is. An. Opportunity. For U. If you're willing to see it that way.

All my love,
Daddy

What if you're following a map to somewhere you don't want to go?

(DAY 194)

Dear Girls,

There's a lie we learn early, one that sounds noble enough to believe: Say yes. Be helpful. Be available. Be everything for everyone.

But here's what I've learned: Always saying yes to others today means saying no to your future self tomorrow.

We don't realize it right away. We think we're being kind. Flexible. Responsible. But we're actually trading away our time in tiny, silent increments. In trying to please others, we punish ourselves, burying our potential to meet someone else's expectations.

We chase another person's definition of success and call it

ambition. But all it creates is confusion disguised as productivity. Some call it a lack of self-awareness. Society just calls it winning.

Let me tell you about a morning that changed me. I had just finished an early coffee meeting. It was 8:06. I didn't have anything scheduled until lunch. Normally, I'd go home or bury myself in work. But that morning, I didn't check my calendar. I didn't open my email. I didn't even glance at a to-do list.

Instead, I rolled the windows down and drove. No GPS. No destination. Just a morning of aimless intention. The air was crisp, and fall had finally arrived. The kind of crisp that wakes you up gently. The trees were the same. The sky hadn't changed. But somehow, everything looked brighter, or maybe I was finally *seeing* it. Birds chirped through the open window. They weren't any louder than usual. They'd always been there. I just hadn't been listening.

For the first time in weeks, I remembered: The emails could wait. The pings, the updates, the opinions would all still be there when I got home. But this moment? This breath? This window-down clarity? I *needed* this. It wasn't an escape. It was a return.

Halfway through the drive, the irony hit me: *I was choosing to wander for a morning. Most people wander their entire lives.*

We'd never open Google Maps without a destination. We'd never just type in "anywhere" and start driving, hoping it worked itself out. Yet most of us drift through our days exactly like that—busy, moving, checking off lists. All without ever naming where we actually want to go. We demand precision from our phones, but we tolerate vagueness in our own souls. And then we wonder why we end up lost. We follow the noise. We follow pressure. We follow comparison. If life threw us a detour, would we even know?

A detour only exists when you've set a direction. And again, maybe the road you're on was never really yours. I don't have all the answers.

You won't always know where you're headed, but I can tell you this: Don't be afraid to pause. To roll the windows down. To check your soul's compass instead of your phone.

Sometimes, the most important direction in life is the one that leads you back to yourself.

All my love,
Daddy

Are you brave enough to face the questions that unsettle your soul?

(DAY 199)

Dear Girls,

Most people think they're afraid of the answers. But it's the questions that do the real damage.

They're quiet at first. They show up when it's dark. They tug at the edge of your comfort. And then, one day, they sit across from you like an old friend you forgot how to recognize. What shocked me the most this year was how loud the silence became when I didn't have a phone to scroll.

When the noise faded, the questions came. Not brand new ones. They were more like old truths that had been trying to reach me for years. But I never gave them enough space to grow. Every time something sharp rose to the surface—a thought, a memory, a question that pierced too deep—I used to reach for the screen. I'd drown it in a scroll. Numb it with noise. But this year? There was nowhere to run.

One night, I remember standing in line at the grocery store, just waiting. No text to check. No feed to scroll. I looked around, and everyone else was looking down.

And then it hit me: *If this was the last day of my life, would I be proud of how I spent it?*

I didn't like the answer. But I couldn't look away.

That's what these questions are. Not just thoughts. Not just ideas. They're mirrors. And they don't show you who you *pretend* to be. They show you who you actually are.

Here are some of the questions that came to visit me as I drove home from the grocery store:

- *What if I'm waiting for permission no one can give me?*
- *I update my phone the moment Apple tells me to—but when was the last time I updated my mindset?*
- *How would I listen if this was the last conversation I ever had with someone I love?*
- *If someone aired my life like a documentary, what moments would I beg them to cut?*
- *If every hour of my day was billed to my purpose, how much would be marked "wasted"?*
- *What lies do I still tell myself just to get through the day?*
- *What am I carrying that isn't mine anymore?*
- *Do I want to be liked, or do I want to be free?*

- *What if I already have all the information I need, and the only thing missing is the courage to act?*
- *What's the question I'm most afraid to ask?*

One day, you'll have to ask your own questions.

Girls, I don't know my answers yet and I won't pretend to know yours. I'm not supposed to. This book isn't a guidebook. It's a map back to your own inner voice.

You don't have to answer all the questions. But please don't run from the ones that make you feel something. That's where the gold is. The questions that unsettle your soul? Those are the ones that start the fire.

All my love,
Daddy

What do you do with someone else's noise?

(DAY 206)

Dear Girls,

This morning, I got cut off in traffic. Not a little lane drift. A full-on "what-is-this-guy-doing" kind of move. He was driving like he was trying to qualify for the Indy 500—except it was December, and qualifications for Indy only happen in May.

Part of me wanted to lay on the horn. Part of me wanted to chase him down, roll down the window, and ask, "What could possibly be that important?"

Maybe he was responding to emails. Maybe he was checking Facebook, texting a coworker, or setting his fantasy football lineup. Or maybe he just got the worst news of his life. Maybe he was rushing to say goodbye to someone he loved. Maybe he was late for a year-end review that held his job in the balance. Maybe he was still seething from fighting with his wife that morning or sitting in shame from a promotion he didn't get. Maybe.

But here's what probably happened: He hit snooze. Twice. Then, he reached for his phone. Scrolled through news, noise, and other people's curated lives. Still in bed. No need for him to eat breakfast because he was already full of other people's opinions. In ten minutes, he went from unconscious to completely reactive and then got behind the wheel of a car.

The real truth? I wasn't mad at him. I was disappointed in myself. Disappointed that I let him shape my morning. Disappointed that I gave him that kind of power over my peace. I had unintentionally handed him the keys to much more than a car. I permitted him to sit in my thoughts long after he sped away. That's the part I'm working on. Because in a distracted world, everyone's chaos is trying to become your chaos. Everyone's urgency is knocking on your peace. Everyone's noise is asking your attention to bend toward it.

Here's what I want you to know: You don't have to pick up what someone else drops. You don't have to carry what wasn't meant for you. That driver was living in a storm. And for a moment, I let the wind in. But now I see it clearer. It's not him. It's me. It's what I choose to hold onto. It's the space where I give my thoughts to grow. It's how I show up in the silence after the noise.

That's where peace lives. Not in controlling the world, but in controlling what gets to come with you.

So if you ever find yourself rattled by someone else's recklessness or spinning from a stranger's storm...pause. Breathe. Bless them, and keep moving.

That's what I'll try to do, too.

All my love,
Daddy

What if this has nothing to do with a phone?

Dear Girls,

It was only three weeks in, but it already felt like something deeper had begun. Just a simple walk with a notebook in my back pocket. I wasn't chasing steps or trying to clear my head. I was just...out there. Sunshine. Breathing. Moving. Paying attention.

Before this journey began, I had spent six weeks obsessing over it. Spreadsheets, blog ideas, structure, and even possible titles for a book I hadn't yet lived. I was giddy in my office, thinking of all the angles. I must've scribbled down fifty potential titles, some clever, some cheesy, most too soon. I was building the scaffolding before the foundation. I wanted to make the year matter before letting it speak.

But this walk? This walk interrupted all of that. Somewhere along the sidewalk, between the crunch of leaves and the silence that had finally started to settle in my bones, I heard it. Not out loud. Not booming from the clouds. Just quietly, like something I'd always known but finally remembered:

What if this has nothing to do with a phone? I stopped walking. It wasn't just a question. It was a shift.

Then, another whisper: *If you think this was your idea, think again.* And just like that, I knew.

I hadn't turned off my phone to be more productive. Or more impressive. Or to win some invisible badge of presence. I had turned it off because God wanted my attention. And not just for five minutes of morning prayer while I sipped coffee. He wanted all of me. My focus. My fear. My longing. My ache. My hours. This wasn't about distraction anymore. It was about devotion.

And then came the last whisper. Not a command. Not a demand. Just a gentle offering: *You can come up with those cute titles, but here's the one I think works:* **Answering the Call...Without Your Phone.**

I didn't need a whiteboard. I didn't need a content calendar. I just needed to listen. And maybe that's the lesson I'll take with me—not just from that walk, but from this year. That the voice of God isn't loud. It's loving. And it doesn't shout over the noise; it waits in the silence.

Girls, I want you to remember this: You don't need a retreat, a sabbatical, or a radical challenge to hear from God.

You just need to stop long enough to listen. Because He's always speaking. Even on quiet sidewalks. Even in the middle of our big, messy questions. Even when we think we already know the plan.

You might go looking for a book title. But sometimes, you'll find your calling instead.

All my love,
Daddy

How much is enough?

Dear Girls,

I wrestle with something I've never quite had the courage to name until now. It's this constant tug-of-war between being present and providing more. You'll get physical things along the way, but I'll always want to give you more experiences. Adventures. Opportunities. Life.

I want to give you the world. And at the same time, I want to be there for the small, ordinary, sacred moments that make up your world.

This tension is something I've carried long before either of you could say "Daddy." It's part of my DNA, this drive to work hard, build something from nothing, and show you that discipline and commitment can create a life filled with possibility.

But this year, without a phone, without the constant hum of more, I started to notice something: The best moments didn't come from planning. They didn't come from the grand gestures or the big trips. They came from spontaneity. From flexibility. From the moments that didn't care what time it was.

Like going to get ice cream on a Tuesday night just because it sounded like fun.

Or playing tag in the backyard even though bedtime was ten minutes ago. Moments that didn't appear on a calendar or get posted on social media yet burrowed themselves deep into my soul. That's the paradox I've come to live in.

I want to provide for you, not just today but years from now. And I want to build something with my life that gives you options, that says, "Your dad didn't just talk about dreams; he chased them."

But here's what I'm learning: *Provision without presence becomes pressure. And presence without provision can feel like fear.*

So the balance? It's not about giving you everything. It's about giving you the right things.

And here's what that looks like: I'm all there when I'm at work, whether on stage, in a meeting, or writing words like these. Not torn. Not distracted. Not halfway in and halfway aching to be somewhere else. When I'm home, holding your hand, dancing in the kitchen, or tucking you in, I'm not somewhere else in my head, solving problems or strategizing what's next.

Because the truth is, you don't need a dad who's always available; you need a dad who's fully present when it counts.

I promise you this: I'll keep learning where that line is. I'll keep adjusting, listening, and showing up—not perfectly, but intentionally. Because one of the biggest lies we're told is that success and presence are mutually exclusive. They're not. But they require constant calibration.

So, if you ever feel me wrestling, know that it's because I love you. Because I want to give you both the roots and the wings. Because I want to show you what it looks like to chase something bigger without ever losing sight of what matters most.

And if you ever wonder, "Daddy, how much is enough?" The answer will always be the same: This. Right here. Right now. Us.

All my love,
Daddy

What am I leaving in you?

DAY 219

Dear Girls,

There's a question that's been following me lately: How am I preparing you to live when I'm not here?

Not someday. Not theoretically. But now. In the way I live. In the choices I make when you're watching—and maybe more importantly, when you're not. How am I preparing you both to step into a messy world and not just survive, but thrive?

I used to focus on what I wanted to leave for you. But this year, I started asking a better question: What am I leaving *in* you? The answer showed up in a quiet moment. We were cleaning up the playroom. Well, *I* was cleaning up the playroom. I was tired, a little irritated, and I just wanted the toys off the floor. Without being asked, Natalia, you looked at me and said, "I'll help, Daddy."

You had no idea what that moment meant to me. You just wanted to help. But you didn't ask if there'd be a reward. You didn't expect applause. You just saw something needed doing, and you stepped in.

Suddenly, I saw her: your grandma. My mom. She wasn't loud with her voice, but her presence carried weight. She never lectured about doing the right thing. She just did it. She didn't make kindness a performance; she made it a practice. She showed me what it meant to show up without being asked.

To help without needing to be thanked. To give without keeping score. And now, you're showing me the same thing without even trying. Which makes me wonder if maybe the river's already flowing through you.

Because life is a river, girls. It moves fast. It gets muddy. And most people stand on the banks, afraid to wade in. They wait for permission. They wait for guarantees. They wait for the water to calm.

But I want to live in a way that teaches you how to jump in. To get your feet wet. To get your hands dirty. To help even when no one's looking.

And that means I can't keep putting things off. Not the hard conversations. Not the dreams. Not the quiet lessons I hope will echo after I'm gone.

Because I believe this more than ever: *Tomorrow* is the most dangerous word in the English language. It promises us there will always be more time. It tricks us into postponing our presence. It gives fear a longer leash. It's how legacies get lost, and how love gets delayed.

So today, I teach. Today, I show up. Today, I wade into the river and let you see me soaked with effort. Because the only way to prepare you for the world that's coming is to be fully present in the one we're in.

I love you more than these words will ever carry. But maybe, if I write them well enough, you'll still feel me in them long after I'm gone.

All my love,
Daddy

What did she teach me about presence?

(DAY 228)

Dear Girls,

I want to tell you about someone who knows how to show up before I knew what that phrase meant. My mom, your grandma. Nana.

She doesn't read mindfulness books. She doesn't listen to podcasts on presence. She doesn't go on retreats, practice yoga, or download meditation apps. But she is the most present person I've ever known.

She doesn't talk about being in the moment; she lives there. Fully. Quietly. Steadily.

She has this way of making people feel like they matter. Like the room gets warmer just because she is in it. Not in a flashy way. Not to get noticed. She just notices you. Notices the little things that most people miss—the sigh, the slumped shoulders, the silence that meant something is off. She stops folding laundry just to sit across from me at the table if she senses something is on my heart. She asks if I am okay. If I don't answer, she waits. Not with pressure. Just with love.

That's what presence is. It's not about perfection. It's about proximity. It's about being near enough to notice the stuff that doesn't get said.

Girls, she believes in me in a way no one else ever has, even before I believe in myself. When I was younger, probably close to your age, I'd come up with these big dreams. I wanted to be a referee, a fireman, and a security guard. And where some parents might nod politely or smile and wait for the phase to pass, she leans in.

She says, "You can do anything you put your mind to, Tommy." Not because I have the credentials. But because she sees something in me.

After getting hired to officiate in D1 Men's College Basketball, she gave me a book congratulating me on my accomplishment. She wrote on the inside cover with her familiar, slanted handwriting:

Tom, You can achieve your dreams. Always think positive and big and it will be yours. Love, Mom.

I still have that book. Not because the book changed my life, but because she did. Because those words weren't just a pep talk. They were a promise, a mother's quiet declaration: I see you. I believe in you. You're meant for more.

You'll have a lot of people in your life who try to measure your worth. They'll look at what you've accomplished. What you've posted. What you've bought. What you've built. But your Grandma sees through all of that. She sees the becoming, even when it is still messy and incomplete. And now, I try to carry that into how I love you.

If I ever pause while unloading groceries just to listen to you tell a long story about school...if I ever stay up a little too late because you can't sleep and just want to talk...if I ever pull you in close without asking questions...it's because your Grandma taught me how.

This whole year without a phone? This whole journey of listening deeper and living slower? It didn't start with me turning something off. It started with me remembering her. What she models. What she believes. What she hands down, without ever making it a lesson.

She is presence in motion. She is kindness without an agenda. She is the quiet faith that never needs a spotlight.

And I see her in you. In your laughter. In your silliness. In your big hearts and messy questions.

If there ever comes a day when the world tries to convince you that you're only valuable when you're doing more, remember her. Remember how she stays. How she makes space. How she never rushes the moment.

Because presence, girls, isn't a trend. It's a legacy. And hers is alive in you.

All my love,
Daddy

How can you feel heard if you never listen to yourself?

(DAY 236)

Dear Girls,

One of the deepest longings we carry as humans is the desire to be heard. But here's the part no one talks about: How can you feel heard if you never give yourself the silence to listen?

I realized that I didn't avoid silence because it's boring; I avoided it because it's honest. When you've built your life on motion, noise, and achievement, stillness feels like failure. Presence feels like a threat.

I think about the part of me that didn't go on this journey. The version that kept checking boxes. Replying to emails. Cranking out results. Being "on top of things."

That version wasn't evil. He wasn't cruel. But he was hollow. He didn't know how to listen to anything except urgency. He didn't know how to measure anything except productivity. Worst of all, he didn't know he was drifting because he was so busy keeping up.

Here's the thing I want you to remember: You can't feel seen when you're hiding behind a full calendar. You can't feel heard when your soul is buried under to-do lists. You can't feel alive when every moment is lived for someone else's validation.

I was raised not to process emotions but to get results. To provide, not to pause. To lead, not to listen. So I moved. I hustled. I achieved. And when the stillness finally came with this journey, I panicked. Because the quiet is where the truth lives. If you've ignored your soul long enough, it sounds like a stranger.

During this year, I met that stranger—not because I'm better than anyone else, but because I finally gave myself the gift of enough silence to hear what he had to say. He was tired. Lonely. Ashamed. Still hopeful. He didn't want a break. He wanted a return. Not to the grind, but to himself.

That's what I want for you, girls. Not a life of constant doing, but a life rooted in being. In truth. In presence. I want you to know how to sit with your own heart. To listen when it speaks. To rest without guilt. To create margin for meaning, not just movement.

And here's what I'm still learning: Just because my phone's off doesn't mean the noise is gone. I have to choose silence. Not as a punishment. But as protection. As recharging.

We plug in our phones multiple times daily to recharge, but when was the last time we plugged back into our soul? A calendar full of meetings doesn't prove your worth. It just proves you're busy. And maybe it's not even the kind of busy you want to be.

So, girls, if you ever find yourself aching to be heard, start by sitting still. Not with your phone. Not with your fears. But with yourself. That's where the voice lives. And when you honor it, God will meet you there.

All my love,
Daddy

What if the judgment isn't about them?

(DAY 240)

Dear Girls,

It happened early in the journey during the second week. We were at the park. You were both running, climbing, and laughing. And then I saw him: a dad, just like me, with two girls, just like you. Five o'clock in the evening on a Saturday. And there he was...on his phone.

I watched him thumb through something, his face lit by a glow that wasn't the sun. And something inside me snapped. I wanted to walk over, rip the phone out of his hand, smash it against the pavement, and yell, "Wake up! What could possibly be more important than *this moment?*"

My hands clenched. My jaw locked. My chest tightened like my heart didn't trust me with it anymore. I was irritated. No, I was furious. Like rage had been living under my skin, just waiting for a reason to release. And now here it was, aimed at a stranger, who was probably just tired, just human, just surviving.

Anger doesn't care about reason. Anger wants release. And that day, I wanted to make someone pay for something I hadn't even fully named yet.

Here's the thing about anger: It's usually covering something softer. Something you don't want to admit.

Later that night, after you were asleep, I sat in the dark. No noise. No distractions. And in the silence, something whispered: *Your reaction wasn't about him.*

That man with his phone? I don't know his story. I don't know if he was texting his boss, checking on a sick parent, or barely holding it together. But I judged him like I knew. Because part of me still needed to punish the version of me I used to be. The one who missed moments like this. The one who thought presence meant proximity. The one who was there, but not *really* there. And so I got angry, because I saw my old reflection in someone else's life.

What I didn't realize in that moment was that I was grieving. Grieving the giggles I ignored while I was refreshing an inbox. Grieving the way I used to scroll through your childhood like it could wait. Grieving the sacredness I traded for productivity.

Girls, this is something I hope you'll always remember: *What we judge in others is often what we're still healing in ourselves.* That moment wasn't about a man and his phone. It was about me and my grief.

So, I'm learning to lead with curiosity instead of critique. With compassion instead of comparison. That moment taught me something: It's easy to judge. It's harder to look inward. And only one of those two actions will change your life.

All my love,
Daddy

What if presence is the new rebellion?

(DAY 246)

Dear Girls,

There is a national epidemic, and we are all infected. It's not airborne. It's ambient. You can't hear it, but you can feel it. If you sit in a coffee shop long enough, you'll watch it unfold in real-time.

People everywhere with their eyes cast downward. Thumbs twitching like they're trying to keep a secret from the rest of the body. And the only thing more surprising than how often we check our phones is how often we don't even realize we're doing it.

It's not just a habit; it's muscle memory at this point. Like blinking. Like breathing. Like grabbing your keys, forgetting why you walked into the room, or saying "I'm fine" when you're anything but. We don't even call it addiction because everyone's doing it. And when everyone's doing it, it just becomes "life."

I need you to know this: Every time we choose our phone over the person in front of us, we're making a small withdrawal from the bank of real connection. And those withdrawals add up. Sometimes, someone will say, "But my phone's face-down on the table." And I get it. I used to think that was polite, too. But here's what putting that little rectangle face-down on the table is really saying: "I'm here...kind of. But I'm also on call. If the world calls, you might lose me."

It's a fragile way to love someone. A fragile way to live.

When you both were babies and you were crying, pacifiers would save the day. Even if we didn't know what was the source of your crying, you got a pacifier. Our phones have turned into the adult pacifier. We don't suck on it, but we reach for it just the same. When we're tired, we check. When we're anxious, we check. When we're bored, we check. When we're awkward, we check. When we're waiting in line, we check. When we're feeling lonely, we check. When we're walking into a room full of people, we check. As if the world inside that screen has the answer to the ache inside our chest.

But it doesn't. It never has. And the longer I went without a phone, the more I realized the ache was the invitation. Not something to run from. Not something to numb. But something to sit with. And sitting with something, without reaching for a distraction, has become the new rebellion.

Let's be real: Being here, fully here, is now an act of courage. Presence has become rare—so rare, it's sacred.

That's the kind of person I want to be. That's the kind of dad

I want to be. The kind who looks people in the eye. Who asks how someone's doing—really doing—and has time to listen. The kind who doesn't need a camera to remember a moment. Because the moment was fully lived. Fully felt.

Girls, here's the truth: You can't love someone well when half of you is elsewhere. You can't grow when your roots don't touch the soil of *now*. And you can't be free when you're tethered to a slot machine that lives in your pocket.

In a world full of ghosts hiding behind screens, the most radical thing you can do is show up and be there.

All my love,
Daddy

What if everything got louder when I unplugged?

DAY 254

Dear Girls,

The first day without a phone was quiet. Not just outside, but also *inside*. The kind of quiet that feels like standing in a room after someone's slammed the door and left.

And in that stillness, I noticed something strange: Everything got louder. Your laughter outside while hitting tennis balls. The crunch of gravel under your scooters. The way butterflies zigzagged like they've never known a destination. Life turned up the volume the moment I turned down the distractions.

We played outside for hours that day. And I watched you live. Fully, innocently, beautifully. And I kept thinking: *Why does everything feel like it's in slow motion?* It was like God came down, put His hands on my shoulders, looked me in the eyes, and froze the frame. Like He was saying, *Don't miss this. Don't forget this. This is what you've been scrolling past.*

Later that night, I sat down and wrote: "Maybe the cell phone was a metaphor. I'm not sure what for, but what is it trying to tell me?"

And that question led me here: What if this journey has nothing to do with a cell phone? What if the phone was just the boarding pass, not the destination?

When we go on vacation, we pull out our phone and scan the boarding pass at the gate. Once we're seated, it's useless. No one walks off the plane, still clutching their boarding pass at the beach. It served its purpose the moment it got us where we were going.

That's what my phone became. The thing I had to surrender so I could take this seat. On this flight. Toward presence. Toward awareness. Toward everything I'd been missing in plain sight.

And here's the thing about boarding passes: You can't use the same one to get back. You need a new one. Because you're never returning as the same person.

So, if you ever have something in your life that feels essential, but is keeping you from really being where you are, ask yourself: *Is this my boarding pass?*

Maybe it was never about the phone. Maybe it was always about where it could take me. Perhaps the cost of presence is finally letting go of what got you here.

All my love,
Daddy

What if courage can't wait?

DAY 262

Dear Girls,

Before we go any further, there's something deeply personal I need to share with you: I have zero expectations that anyone else will do what I did. I'm not writing this to convince you or anyone to turn off your phone for a day, a week, a month, or a year. This was something I chose.

And it's not a badge of honor. It's not a checklist for a better life. It's the unique path I had to tread because I had lost touch with my own heart.

And if we're being honest? I picked the worst possible time to disappear from the world without a cell phone. As you know, your mom was still grieving from losing her mom just a year earlier. You two were still so young, needing me in ways I couldn't always predict. I had just launched my own business less than two years before. Your grandpa's health was fragile.

Life was already demanding more from me than I knew how to give. And still, I went for it.

I didn't wait for a quieter season. I didn't wait for everything to feel convenient, safe, or "smart." I turned off my cell phone for 365 days. Everyone had an opinion. Some laughed. Some mocked. Some supported.

That's okay. I wasn't looking for permission. Because the truth is: There's never a perfect time to wake up. There's never a convenient time to choose a different life. There's only now.

And sometimes, the bravest thing you can do is risk being misunderstood to become someone you can recognize when the noise dies down.

That's what this year was really about. Not perfection. Not protest. Only Presence.

All my love,
Daddy

What if anger is part of the healing?

DAY 269

Dear Girls,

I got angry this year. Not at God. Not at the world. At me.

I was angry that it took me forty years to finally see what matters. Angry that I could be successful, admired, accomplished, and still miss the marrow of my own life. Angry that I spent years preaching about chasing dreams and inspiring others while leaving parts of my own soul untapped.

The anger masked my potential, which left me feeling like a bald eagle unable to fly—majestic in presence but aching in silence, wings designed to kiss the sky but grounded by something invisible. Maybe doubt. Maybe fear. Or maybe a past that clipped the eagle's feathers before it ever learned how to stretch them.

I stood on stages talking about "maximizing your life," but in the silence I had to ask myself: Am I living mine? Am I doing what I ask others to do? Am I showing up fully when no one is watching? Or only when there's applause?

I don't think I've been a bad husband. Or father. Or man. But I also think that's the trap: comparing your life to what it could be worse than instead of what it was meant to be. And the deeper truth? Sometimes, that realization doesn't feel like revelation. It feels like rage. I wanted to scream: Why didn't I know this earlier? Why didn't I change sooner? And I'll never have an answer to that.

I do know this: God's timing isn't always fast, but it's always perfect. Maybe I wasn't ready five years ago. Maybe my soul needed to be worn down a little before it could be rebuilt. Maybe the silence had to feel sharp before it could feel sacred.

Perhaps this anger is not a curse, but a blessing in disguise. It could be the catalyst for a profound transformation, a journey from anger to acceptance, from grief to grace. Maybe it's grief in disguise. Because anger, when you trace it to its root, often leads to mourning. Mourning the life you could have lived. The moments you missed. The days you rushed. The father you were too distracted to be.

Real grace doesn't live in the past; it meets you in the mirror. In the morning, you wake up and say: "I want to do better. Not just when it's easy. Not just when I'm inspired. But every day. Especially when I'm tired. Especially when no one's watching."

That's where the anger starts to change into fire. Purpose. And Presence.

So yes, I got angry this year. But I didn't stay there. I let it show me what I had been blind to. I let it scrape the rust off the places I'd neglected. And then I let it go.

I can't write a book about presence and still live in regret. I can't offer you my truth and still cling to who I was before it broke me open.

Girls, if you ever feel that heat in your chest—not at someone else, but at yourself—I want you to remember this: In the midst of your anger, you are not broken. You are a work in progress. You are waking up to your own potential and power. And if it hurts, good. That means you're alive.

When the anger comes, don't push it away. Let it in. Pull out a chair. Let it tell you about your pain, your regrets, and your unfulfilled potential. Let it tell you the truth.

Then let it pass, so the real work can begin. The work of showing up. Again and again. Even when it's hard. Especially then.

All my love,
Daddy

What if time is shorter than we think?

(DAY 274)

Dear Girls,

Every year around the same time, I take a trip with Nana and Grandpa to the Mayo Clinic in Rochester, Minnesota. Grandpa was diagnosed with Parkinson's five years ago, and this visit has become our annual ritual. Part routine, part reminder that nothing in life stays the same forever.

This year was different, though. Not in dramatic ways. In quiet ones.

The morning we arrive, the hotel's fire alarm goes off. Grandpa and I file outside with the rest of the guests: half-awake, half-irritated. But Nana? She finds the humor in it. She starts chatting with the firemen like they are old friends. Cracking jokes, asking questions, offering to buy lunch for the entire crew and have them come inside to eat. Never mind that their two firetrucks are parked haphazardly across the main entrance like this is a full-on emergency.

Grandpa just shakes his head, quietly mortified. I laugh beside her. She doesn't care what anyone thinks. She is just...Nana. Making the ordinary absurd. And holy.

Later that day, we sit together in the doctor's office—Nana, Grandpa, and me, all three of us facing the neurologist. I happen to be sitting where I can see them, too, and as I watch them nod and ask questions, something happens. I see it. Like a flash forward. A fast glimpse of the future. Thirty years from now, sitting in chairs just like these. You two across from me, shoulders older, eyes wiser, offering emotional support, trying to steady yourselves as we work to make sense of a diagnosis that might change everything.

I swallow hard. In that moment, I don't just see the future. I feel it. And I find myself wondering: *Am I becoming the kind of man you'd want to sit beside? If this were us someday, would you feel proud to be there? Or burdened?*

It makes me want to work harder—not for applause, not for success, but for legacy. The kind that isn't stored in a bank account or a résumé, but in the *way you love through uncertainty.* It makes me want to become the kind of father whose life gives you courage, not just comfort.

I start thinking about the next thirty years. What kind of women will you become? What kind of world will you inherit? What kind of example will I have left?

I don't care if you change the world on a stage with a micro-
phone. I just hope you change your corner of it. With your
hands, heart, words, and presence. I hope you believe you're
capable of hard things. I hope you know you can always take
one more step. I hope you forgive others when it's inconvenient.
I hope you take care of your people.

That's what this trip to Mayo reminds me: not that time is
running out, but that it's *ours*—and it's precious.

Sometimes, the most sacred moments are the ones where nothing significant happens...except that you *see* your life clearly
for a second.

That vision of the future? It isn't scary. It is sobering. And clar-
ifying. And it whispered a question I'll keep asking as long as
I have breath: *What if it's my turn next?* And if it is—if someday
I'm in that chair, hands trembling, mind fading—I hope I've
lived in a way that makes you want to show up. Not out of duty.
But out of love.

All my love,
Daddy

What if you never read these letters?

DAY 279

Dear Girls,

There's a question I keep circling, even as I write to you day after day, pouring ink into paper like it might keep me close to you long after I'm gone.

What if you never read these letters? What if, after all my good intentions, this book never gets published? What if the pages get lost in a drawer or sit untouched on a dusty shelf? What if life moves too fast, and you're too busy living to look back? Would the words still matter?

I used to think the most important thing I could do was say what I believed. But this year taught me something different: What matters most is what you see. What you see in my eyes when I'm looking at you instead of a screen. What you see in how I treat your mother. What you see when I hold open a door for a stranger. When I apologize. When I fall short. When I get back up.

Maybe these letters are more than words; maybe they're reminders. But not for you. For me. A kind of quiet confession. A way of telling God: "I don't need to be in control anymore." Because control was killing something soft in me.

This year without a phone, without constant scrolling, without the illusion of being needed 24/7, was where I learned how to surrender. Not just my schedule. Not just my scrolling. But my identity.

That's why even if you never read a single word of this book, I'll keep living like you did. Because the truest values don't need to be preached. They need to be practiced. To love God. To be kind to others. To speak up. To stay soft. To respect your parents, your neighbors, your bodies, your silence. And above all, yourselves.

You'll hear people say that legacy is what we leave behind. But I think legacy is what we live out in front of the people we love. Moment by moment. Breath by breath. Not with grand declarations, but with the small daily choices that quietly declare: *This is who I am. This is what I believe.*

This is what I hope you'll carry, e if you never read the letters. Even if my words never reach your eyes. My prayer is that you'll feel them in your bones. In the bedtime kisses. In the belly laughs. In the mornings when I mess up and try again. In the red light gratitude game. In the way I keep showing up.

Because love doesn't need an audience. It just needs a vessel.

This journey? It isn't over when the book ends. The letters may stop, but the becoming continues. One day, when you write your own story, I hope you won't need my words to know where it all began.

All my love,
Daddy

What if I followed through?

(DAY 282)

Dear Girls,

I need to tell you something I never planned to say out loud. Because if I had followed through, you wouldn't be reading this.

One night, I sat on my office floor and wrote a note. My hands shook as I folded it into a small, uneven square and tucked it in the back of my desk drawer. It said:

> *You all got your wish. I didn't finish my year without a cell phone. Tell Giuliana and Natalia I'm sorry. Tell them I love them.*

That was it.

That night, I couldn't see past the dark isolation. I wasn't thinking about poetry or presence or peace. I was thinking about the weight. Every day felt like an 800-pound gorilla pressing on my chest, and I didn't know how much longer I could hold it up.

But even heavier than that gorilla was the weight of everyone else's expectations, what I thought I needed to be and was failing to become. The silence I thought I wanted was louder than I expected.

It echoed with questions I didn't want to answer. Questions about who I was when nobody was watching—whether I mattered if I wasn't performing, producing, or proving. And I need you to know: It wasn't a passing thought.

I didn't come to that place all at once. It had been circling me quietly for weeks, like a shadow that grew darker every time someone asked, "How are you?" To which I smiled and said, "I'm fine." And "fine," I've learned, is often a soft, unspoken invitation. It's how we quietly say "help me" without having to break the rules of polite conversation.

There was a plan. I had thought through the logistics. My car would be going at a high rate of speed. I had the tree picked out. I knew where it was. I had driven past it. I knew I would never do anything at home for fear that you girls might find me.

That was unthinkable. But this? This felt...clean. Quiet. Not painless, but less painful than living like this. I didn't want to die. I just wanted the pain to stop. I wanted the pressure to let up. I wanted someone to say, "You don't have to hold the whole world anymore."

And here's what I didn't know, not yet. A few days later, your grandmother had a doctor's appointment. That appointment changed everything. It was the first time we saw something that might be really wrong.

Less than two weeks later, she would be admitted to the ER. She would never come home. She spent 106 days in the hospital. That's not a poetic number. That's not a neat arc. That's a long, slow, brutal goodbye.

I counted every beep of the IV machine. I learned how to sleep upright. I held her hand and kissed her forehead more times in those 106 days than in the last forty years combined.

Somehow, in that moment, before we knew what was coming, something in me shifted. It's my only explanation for why I didn't follow through. There was something in the air that day. Something in my gut. Something in the quiet. It was like your grandmother was speaking to me, but not with words. Like her soul already knew what was ahead. And she was saying: "Stay. I'm going to need you. Your girls will need you. Your dad will need you." And I did.

I didn't feel brave. I felt cornered. And yet something in me, maybe the part still tethered to love, chose to stay. Not because the pain disappeared. Not because I had a revelation. But because love asked me to.

Love, the love I have for you, for your grandmother, for our family—it was that love that gave me the strength to stay. That love showed me the power of resilience and the transformative nature of connection. Because when someone you love is about to enter the most brutal fight of their life, you don't leave.

You show up. Even with shaking hands, an empty cup, or even your heart held together by threads. You show up because they need you more than you need an exit.

Something else happened—something strange and sacred: The fear lost its grip. It was still there, but it wasn't in charge anymore.

Here's the truth I want you to remember when you feel swallowed up by your own darkness: Fear thrives when you're the center of your world. But the second you start living for someone else, it begins to shrink. I don't say this to be noble. I'm not proud of that moment on the floor, but I'm not ashamed.

It taught me something that changed my life: The part of me that wanted to disappear wasn't broken. It was begging for someone to say, "You're allowed to fall apart. But not alone. Not today."

I can't help but wonder if that someone was her. Maybe she gave me just enough reason to hold on a little longer. Maybe she whispered: "You can rest later. Right now, I need you."

Somewhere deep down, even through exhaustion and fear, I realized: I could've missed this. I could have missed holding her hand. I could have missed being there when it mattered most. I could have missed the sacredness hidden inside the sorrow.

And if I had followed through, girls, I would have missed you, too. I would have missed late-night snuggles when your hair still smelled like shampoo and your breath was warm against my chest. I would have missed walking you to the bus stop in oversized backpacks and mismatched socks. I would have missed our first daddy/daughter dance. I would have missed cheering from the sidelines while you learned how to lose with grace and win with kindness. I would have missed that one rainy night when you finally told me the truth about your broken heart. I would have missed the way your faces will change when you fall in love, how your eyes will hold both wonder and terror. I would have missed walking you down the aisle, my heart pounding with pride and the ache of letting go. I would have missed the sound of your babies calling me Grandpa for the first time. I would have missed the days when you'll call just to say, "Hey, I miss you, Dad." I would have missed growing old with you in my life, watching you become women who are brave enough to feel deeply, and gentle enough to keep choosing love anyway.

So, I did the only thing I could. I started showing up. One day, one visit, one goodbye at a time. One morning, I sat beside her bed for six hours without saying a word. I just held her hand. And somehow, that felt like the most honest thing I'd ever done.

You were my reason, too, girls. You just didn't know it. The thought of you finding that note was unbearable.

And that, too, saved me.

All my love,
Daddy

What if growth looks different for everybody?

DAY 290

Dear Girls,

There's a letter I've avoided writing. Not because I don't know what to say. But because I know how tender it is.

It's about your mom. And me. And what this year without a phone revealed that I didn't expect.

The truth? Our marriage didn't improve over the course of this year. I wish I could share a story with breakthroughs, closeness, and connection. But that's not the truth. We weren't fighting. We weren't falling apart. But we weren't really reaching for each other, either. It's hard to admit that. Harder still to sit with the possibility that growth sometimes creates space. Not just inside you, but between you and the person who used to feel closest.

I want to tell you I stayed present. That I softened. That I invited her in. Sometimes I did. More times than not, I didn't.

Because I was consumed, girls. Not just with the silence, but also with what it stirred up.

I was unraveling. I was learning to need God in a way I never had before. And I wasn't always available to explain myself.

The further I traveled inward, the harder it became to narrate that journey in real time. And when someone doesn't recognize who you're becoming, they often cling to who you've been. I don't blame her for that. Change is hard to witness when you don't recognize what you see. Especially when you didn't ask for it.

But I need you to know this: Love doesn't always look like alignment. Sometimes, love looks like tension that stays in the room. Sometimes, it's choosing not to walk away when the map makes no sense. Sometimes, it's loving each other through misunderstanding.

That's where we are now. Still in the room. Still figuring it out. Still believing love can hold real tension without resolving it all at once.

And maybe that's the deeper invitation here: not to fix what feels frayed, but to stay present inside of it.

If you ever find yourself in a moment like this, where your growth is real, but your connection is strained, I hope you don't panic. I hope you don't shrink. And I hope you don't shame someone who doesn't yet understand. Just keep telling the truth. With love. With patience. With clarity. Keep showing up, even if the room feels cold.

Because presence is not about performance. It's about honoring the space between what was and what might still be possible.

I don't know where this part of the story ends. But I know that I love your mom. I know I want to keep evolving into a man who is easier to love, and I'm committed to that journey. And I know that telling you the truth, even the hard truth, is one of the ways I do that.

All my love,
Daddy

What if God was always talking but I couldn't hear Him until I got quiet?

(DAY 294)

Dear Girls,

I grew up believing in God. I believed in God because my parents did, and that's how I was raised.

I was a good Catholic school kid with great parents and a clean conscience. We prayed before meals. We went to Mass. We said the right things and tried to do the right things. And I wouldn't change a single part of that upbringing. I hit the lottery with your grandparents. They provided a roadmap for what loving parents should do.

But if I'm honest? Faith back then was more like an expectation than an encounter. It was a rhythm I respected but not a relationship I relied on. I believed in God the way you believe in gravity, something that exists but doesn't feel personal until you fall.

And I was doing just fine on my own. At least, that's what I told myself. I was achieving, building, climbing. I was getting recognition, making money, staying fit, being productive. And I never said this out loud, but my actions spoke for me: Why bother God with anything that wasn't broken?

Turns out, that was the problem. I wasn't falling apart. But I was falling asleep. So when I turned off my phone and finally removed the noise, I didn't expect what happened next.

I thought this would be a year about attention. Focus. Simplicity. Maybe a good story for the next keynote speech. What I didn't expect...was God. Not in the distant, polite sense. But in the living, breathing, undeniably present kind of way that was uniquely mine.

The first day I turned off my phone was the same day we started going to Northview Church. The timing wasn't orchestrated. Not consciously, anyway. But now I look back and wonder if maybe God was waiting for me to make enough space. Just enough silence. Just enough surrender.

And once I did? Once I laid down the control, the performance, the curated importance of my screen, He whispered: *Finally. Are you ready now?*

Girls, I didn't give up my phone to find God. But once I turned it off, I could finally hear Him. Here's what I've learned: God never stopped speaking. He never stopped guiding. He never stopped loving. He was just waiting for me to stop filling the space with my own voice. I can't promise that this would happen to another person who turned their phone off, but it's what happened to me.

This whole journey was never about a phone. That was just the boarding pass.

A way to get on the plane. A way to begin. But the real destination? It was intimacy. Stillness. Obedience. Not because God needed me to perform for Him, but because He was ready to partner with me. That's the surprising part. The part I didn't see coming.

This wasn't a year of detox. It was a year of devotion. And the most unexpected moment? God met me right where I was. And God met me there not with shame, but with grace. Not with a scolding, but with an invitation. He said, *You've had your season of striving. Now, let's walk together.*

Girls, I've accomplished a lot in my life. I've reffed big games. I've stood on big stages. But nothing has changed me more than when I realized I don't need to be in control to be held. This year taught me that God isn't an emergency contact, like someone you call only when you're in trouble. He's not a last resort, like a backup plan when everything else fails. He's the source, the foundation of our lives, the one we should turn to first in all situations.

And I say this to you not as a preacher, but as a father who isn't perfect—as someone who has made mistakes yet finally decided to stop trying to do it all on his own: There is a God who knows you. Who hears you. Who loves you more than you will ever comprehend. And He doesn't need you to perform. He just wants you to come home, to find peace and comfort in His presence, to feel the warmth of His love, and to know that you are always welcome in His embrace.

So yes, this journey changed my presence. But more than that? It changed my posture. I don't need the credit anymore. I don't need the spotlight. I just want to be faithful, to live my life in a way that honors God, to be true to His teachings, and to follow His guidance in all that I do.

If this book says anything, I hope it says this: I gave up my phone. But what I found...was God.

All my love,
Daddy

What if coming back feels lonelier than leaving?

(**DAY 298**)

Dear Girls,

There's something no one talks about when they talk about transformation.

They tell you how brave it is to leave. They applaud your courage to let go, strip away, listen to the silence, and shed your old skin. But they don't tell you this: Coming back can feel lonelier than leaving.

What happens when you've changed but no one else has? What happens when the people who love you most still call you by the name of your old self? That was the ache I didn't see coming.

When I left, I knew I was walking away from noise. From distraction. From the curated version of me. The ref. The speaker. The guy who could walk into a room and read it like a playbook.

I wasn't pretending. But I was performing in subtle and socially acceptable ways. And when I started waking up and letting the silence begin to remake me, I realized the mask wasn't just for the world. It was for me, too.

So when I came back, and people noticed the difference, I felt like I had to reintroduce myself all over again. Not to strangers. To people I loved. It's okay to feel this way. It's okay to grieve the person you used to be. That's the grief I didn't expect. That's the loneliness I didn't know how to prepare for.

Even now, as I think about the months to come after the year ends, I sometimes wonder: Will they understand this version of me? Will they still respect me? Will they still love me?

The honest answer? Some will. Some won't. And that has to be okay. Because I didn't go into the fire to come back the same. I didn't turn off my phone to become more palatable. I did it to become more present. And if I lose something in the process, let it be someone's approval. Let it be someone's understanding. That's part of the shedding, too.

One day, girls, you'll change in ways others don't understand. You'll return from the wilderness with new eyes and look around and wonder if anyone notices.

And when that day comes, I hope you remember that you don't need others to recognize your transformation for it to be real. Your journey is valid, and your transformation is authentic.

The applause is not the confirmation. Your peace, your inner calm, your sense of self-worth, and your acceptance of your transformation are what truly matter.

This book? It wasn't written to impress the world. It was written to support you and guide you. It was written to hand you a lantern on the darkest of nights.

Because I know there will be nights when you doubt everything. Nights when you wonder if the new you is "too much" or "too different." Nights when you wish you could go back, just to feel understood again.

But I want you to know: You didn't go through all that fire just to fit back into a life that couldn't hold your soul. Remember, the journey is leading you to freedom. You went through it to be free.

And if freedom feels lonely sometimes, that doesn't mean you're doing it wrong. It means you're doing it honestly.

All my love,
Daddy

What happens when you stop reaching for it?

(**DAY 300**)

Dear Girls,

Today marks three hundred days without a cell phone.

Which means...

Three hundred days without using my phone to kill time while waiting for a meeting to start.

Three hundred days without staring at my screen while walking from my car into a building.

Three hundred days without scrolling the internet while standing in line for coffee.

Three hundred days without taking one picture to document the moment I was in.

Three hundred days without reaching for my phone at the first sign of boredom.

Three hundred days without responding to any notification within seconds.

Three hundred days without being distracted while playing with you.

Three hundred days without checking weather updates or sports scores.

Three hundred days without checking emails before getting out of bed.

Three hundred days without using GPS to arrive at my destination.

Three hundred days without touching my phone during any meal.

Three hundred days without ordering anything online at a red light.

Three hundred days without texting and driving.

Three hundred days without the little device that used to own me.

And honestly? I used to think people would think I was crazy. I worried someone would say I was being reckless, self-righteous, or trying to make a scene. But after three hundred days, I'm starting to wonder if this was the sanest thing I've ever done. Maybe going 365 days without a cell phone isn't as dumb as it seemed.

Here's the truth, girls: I don't remember what I missed. But I remember what I found.

I found your eyes looking up at me, not competing with a screen.

I found that time expands when you're not shrinking it between pings and swipes.

I found that I don't need GPS to know where I'm going when I'm not in a hurry to get there.

I found your laughter filling the room—not just bouncing off the walls, but actually landing in my chest.

I found silence that didn't scream and stillness that didn't shame.

I found that no one is tracking how fast I respond, but you're tracking how close I am when you say, "Watch this, Daddy."

I found that boredom is a gift.

Because boredom isn't emptiness; it's a door. And when you don't slam it shut with distraction, something sacred walks in.

So no, I didn't miss anything urgent. But I witnessed a thousand things I would've otherwise missed entirely.

And girls, someday, when the world tells you faster is better, when the pressure to always be reachable tries to outrun your peace, just remember this: Your attention is the most expensive thing you own. Spend it wisely. Because one day, the things you think are urgent will turn out to be invisible. And the things you think can wait...won't.

All my love,
Daddy

What if joy is the bravest surrender of all?

(**DAY 304**)

Dear Girls,

There's something I've been wrestling with lately. Why do adults lose joy? It's not something that happens all at once. Not on your twenty-first birthday or on the day of your first job offer. But slowly. Quietly. Like someone sneaking out the back door of your life and taking the music with them.

I didn't notice it at first. But somewhere along the way, joy became something I had to earn, not something I was allowed to live.

Maybe that's what this year without a phone gave back to me: not just silence, not just clarity, but the kind of joy I'd forgotten. Not the kind people post about. Not the kind you schedule for two weeks in July.

I'm talking about joy that surprises you. The joy that looks like getting ice cream on a Tuesday for no reason. Running through the rain instead of waiting it out. Letting you cover me in stickers just because it made you laugh. That's when I realized something that changed me: Joy isn't childish. It's sacred. It's not what happens when everything is perfect. It's what happens when you stop trying to be.

Girls, I don't know why we lose this as we age. Maybe it's the pressure. Maybe it's bills and emails and being told that seriousness is the same thing as significance.

But I've learned this much: There is nothing more significant than your laughter. There is no accomplishment that means more to me than the sound of you squealing with joy in the backseat. There is no stage I'd rather be on than the floor of your room with a princess crown on my head and a plastic teacup in my hand.

You don't need me to be a referee, a speaker, or "important." You just need me to be with you. Fully. Lightly. Loosely. Playfully. You need me to remember that life isn't always about fixing or producing. Sometimes, it's about dancing in the kitchen.

I'm learning, girls, slowly but surely, that joy is the bravest surrender of all. It's the surrender of the mask. The surrender of control. The surrender of what other people think.

It's hard. Because joy makes you vulnerable. It exposes the softest parts of you. It says: I'm still open. I'm still here. I'm still willing to laugh even after all I've lost.

That's the version of me I want you to remember. Not the

stressed-out version. Not the one rushing to the next meeting. Not the one buried in tasks, barely looking up. I want you to remember this version. The one who stops at every red light just to play the gratitude game. The one who says "yes" to one more dance, one more pancake, one more kiss. The one who knows that the most eternal things are often disguised as ordinary ones.

So here's my promise to you: I won't wait for perfect days to be joyful. I won't keep joy locked in the cabinet of "someday." I'll find it in the cereal aisle. In the sidewalk chalk. In the bedtime stories and grocery store detours.

Because life is too short to keep waiting for permission. Joy is not a luxury. It's a way of being. And the bravest thing I can do is to choose it. Again and again. Even when the world forgets.

Especially when the world forgets.

All my love,
Daddy

What if one day you feel like leaving, too?

Dear Girls,

I've sat with this question more times than I care to admit: What if I can't protect you from what hurts?

And I don't mean scraped knees or broken hearts, though those will come. I mean the deep pain. The kind that makes you question everything. The kind that makes you wonder if there's still enough love in the world to carry you through.

That's what scares me most. Not because I think you'll be fragile. But because I know what it feels like to believe you've run out of reasons to stay.

And I won't be able to fix it, whether I'm in the room, across the world, or already gone. There will be moments when I can't reach you. But my love will. Let this letter be proof of that.

Because here's what I need you to know: There is more love than you can feel right now. More help than you know how to ask for. More light than your darkness will ever understand. You don't have to earn it. You don't have to hide from it. You don't have to figure everything out before you let someone in.

If you ever reach that breaking point, or if you ever feel like disappearing, please wait. Wait one more day. Please open a window. Call someone. Cry until your chest aches. And if you need to scream, scream. But don't go silent. The silence almost took me.

But something, someone called me back. And now, I wonder if it was you. If your little voices were saying, "Stay. We're going to need you." And girls, I stayed. Not because I felt brave. But because love whispered, "Not yet. There's more to do. More to become. More to give."

I can't promise you a pain-free life. But I can promise you this: Pain is not the same as hopelessness. One is part of being human. The other is a lie that wants to steal your joy.

If you ever find yourself in a dark place, a place where it feels like the light will never return, please remember: You are not broken. You are becoming. And becoming is hard. It stretches. It hurts. It burns. But it builds something more substantial.

You will rise—not in spite of the ache, but because of it. When you do, I'll be there, a constant presence in your life. In your bones. In your faith. In your fire. You'll feel me in the stillness after a long cry. In the voice that says, "Keep going." In the warmth that tells you, "You are never beyond love."

My love for you is enduring. Today. Tomorrow. Forever.

All my love,
Daddy

What will I regret?

DAY 313

Dear Girls,

There's a question I've been carrying for months now. It keeps me honest. It whispers when I'm about to take the easy way out. It wakes me up when I'm tempted to sleepwalk through life.

"What will I regret?"

The question is not a tool of fear, but a compass of wisdom. I don't ask it to scare myself. I ask it to anchor myself. Throughout the year, I let this question be the frame for every conversation, every interaction, every speech. To let me think through when something was over and look back with an objective eye.

So, fast-forward to when this year is over. What would I regret?

I'd regret withholding love because I was afraid.

I'd regret playing it safe, so no one could judge me.

I'd regret not giving God full credit for what He walked me through this year.

That's why I've written every word like I'm no longer afraid of what people might think. Because I don't want to live a curated life. I want to live a courageous one.

And that brings me to something tender, girls. One day, someone might read this book and use it against you. They might tease you. Or me. They might say something that feels sharp and unfair. I hate that possibility. I never set out to make you vulnerable by sharing my own vulnerability.

But here's the truth: There will always be people who shame. Who judge. Who hurt others because they're hurting themselves. The courage to face this head-on is a strength that will always protect you. And you can't live your life trying to avoid all of that.

What you can do is ask better questions:

What truly matters to me?

What kind of world do I want to help build?

What will I regret if I don't say or do or create?

Then go do that thing. Even if it costs you something. Especially if it costs you your fear. Because regret is a cost I'm no longer willing to pay.

All my love,
Daddy

What if my kids don't care about my accomplishments?

(**DAY 317**)

Dear Girls,

The night I realized you didn't care that I wrote my first children's book was when I learned what matters.

You were fresh out of the bath, wrapped in towels like little burritos, wild hair dripping on the carpet. The kind of moment where everything is chaos but also perfect. You were picking out bedtime stories, browsing like you were in a bookstore you've been to a hundred times but still want to check every shelf.

"Hey, Giuliana, what books do you want to read tonight?" I asked, fully expecting you to reach for the book I wrote for you. You paused and shrugged.

I offered a suggestion. "Let's read the book I wrote for you."

And you hit me with a one-word thunderclap: "No."

It didn't hurt. It humbled me. I realized in that second that nothing I accomplish in this life will mean as much to you as that I am simply there.

You don't care that your dad wrote a book. You care that I helped you dry your hair. You care that I put the toothpaste on your toothbrush but let you brush your own teeth. You care that I stayed until you fell asleep, listening to your slow, rhythmic breaths in your new big-girl bed.

You reminded me that I could win awards, speak on stages, have initials behind my name, and still miss the whole point. Because presence will always outrank performance.

I used to think success was what other people said about you when you weren't in the room. Now I know it's what your kids remember when you are. And that memory isn't going to be about some big moment.

It's not going to be about the applause. It will be about pancakes on Saturday mornings, the time I got too into coloring, or how I showed up at gymnastics class even though it meant missing a "business call."

You girls have taught me that being there is the most underrated miracle in the world.

So thank you for the "no." You reminded me that things that don't matter don't matter.

All my love,
Daddy

What if a day was enough?

DAY 320

Dear Girls,

If I close my eyes, I can still hear it. The sound of silence, before the sun came up. Before the cereal bowls clinked. Before your tiny footsteps padded across the hall, asking if it was time to get dressed yet.

Time before you wake up has become sacred. Most days, unless I have an early meeting, I don't set an alarm. I find myself waking up before 5:00 a.m., and now I crave the alone time to start the day.

Usually, nothing profound happens during this time. But I began to look forward to it because there was no screen to scroll. No news to catch up on. No inbox or calendar pinging like an impatient child.

Just a notebook. A pen. And silence, thick and alive, like it had something to say if I'd just stay still long enough to listen.

At first, that silence felt empty, like walking into a cavern with nothing but your breath echoing back at you. But over time, and this still surprises me, I got good at sitting with it. Not fixing anything. Not forcing insight. Just being still.

Some mornings, I'd just sip my coffee and stare out the window, letting the light inch across the floor like a quiet invitation. And sometimes, more often than I'd like to admit, I'd just sit there and cry, because stillness has a way of scraping things loose that you've hidden in the busyness.

Then the house would wake up. Toothbrushes would get lost. Pancakes would burn. Hairbrushes would cause tears, and breakfast would be both a battlefield and a banquet.

That, too, became sacred. Because presence doesn't mean serenity. It means choosing to be here, even when "here" is chaotic.

From eight in the morning to noon, I'd write. Sometimes from my home office. Sometimes from a picnic bench in a local park. I did my best thinking in places that didn't require power. Parks don't need a Wi-Fi password. The trees never care if you're essential.

I'd write newsletters. Draft speeches. Try to give shape to this invisible transformation I was undergoing. It was like trying to paint the wind. But I kept showing up, pen in hand, chasing the language that might one day explain it all to you.

Afternoons were quieter. A workout. A walk. Lunch with your mom. Because we both worked from home, we had chances to bump into each other throughout the day, which became its own kind of gift. Not dramatic. Just proximity without performance.

Later, I'd walk to the coffee shop to coach an executive, someone leading a team, managing pressure, wondering if they were enough. And I'd sit across from them, phone-free, with a heart that had been cracked open by the silence, and I'd listen better than I ever did when I had a phone in my pocket. Coaching without distraction taught me something profound: When you look someone in the eye and hold their gaze, you don't need to be impressive. You just need to be present.

At 5:00 p.m., I shut everything down.

That's the goal, anyway.

Does it happen every day? No. But it happens more often than not. And even that is a miracle, because before any behavior changes, something deeper has to happen first: self-awareness. This is the key that empowers us and puts us in control of our transformation.

That's what I'm starting to notice during this year. I'm noticing myself. Not with judgment, but with a sense of wonder and curiosity. I'm beginning to ask harder questions.

Not just "Is this working?" But "Why do I keep doing it this way?" Not just "Am I tired?" But "What am I carrying that I never set down?" And maybe the biggest one: "Have I mistaken being busy for being alive?"

This year is stripping away all the autopilot routines I never questioned before. And I'm learning that transformation doesn't begin with discipline. It begins with *noticing.*

One hour to check and reply to emails, the only time I gave to the outside world's demands. I guarded that boundary like a sentry at the door of my peace. And then...dinner. Baths. Bedtime stories. Giggles and last-minute questions and tiny feet coming in to ask for one more glass of water.

Once you were asleep, I'd return to the silence. Not to *do* anything. Just to *be.*

Because what I've learned is this: A typical day isn't about what fills your calendar. It's about what fills your soul.

You can be busy and still feel hollow. Or you can live a slow, deliberate day and feel as though you've touched eternity. I don't remember the dates. But I remember the *feelings.* And that, I hope, is what you carry.

If you ever find yourself measuring a day by how productive it was, I hope you'll stop and ask a better question:

Did I pay attention?

Because a phone can't teach you that. But a quiet day can.

All my love,
Daddy

What if some things can't be forced, but only allowed?

(DAY 322)

Dear Girls,

Some things, words alone can't carry.

There are moments where you don't just feel pain. You also feel a presence. Something larger than yourself. Something sacred.

The night I returned from the hospital after my heart episode, I felt like I was straddling two worlds. It was a profound moment, and I knew life would never look the same again. My body was back in our house. But my spirit was still in the hospital, asking big questions. Listening for answers.

When I attempted to write down this experience the next day, I found myself at a loss for words. It was as if my hands and mind were not in sync.

Later that night, as I tried to fall asleep, I heard this. I don't know how to explain it, other than to say it felt like God's voice to me. And I want you to have it. To read it when your own heart is heavy. To feel the connection we share through this experience.

Your eyes can only see so far
That's where faith picks up the load
The pain was in your chest which protects your heart
Much like I AM the one who protects your life
The doctors told you it might be a heart attack
Now I'M here to tell you it's time to attack
    this life with your heart
You screamed in pain, "I feel alone"
I whispered in your ear, "I'VE never left your side"
Your heart raced, body shaked, fingers numb
The only thing that never wavers is MY unceasing love
You thought your assignment was over when the
    double doors opened and you saw the light
You asked in a gentle whisper that only I could hear, "Is
    my time here over, am I coming home?"
I placed MY hands on you and reaffirmed,
    "Your journey has just begun"
The weight on your chest squeezed tighter and
    tighter, and at times it felt unbearable
If you should ever worry in the future and
    ask, "O God, where are you?"
Just know you are in MY arms, and MY grip is stronger
    than any physical pain you can endure

The medical staff reassured you that your physical heart is fine
The only thing that needed help was your
  spiritual heart, and that's MINE
When you left the hospital on Sunday
  night, you left something behind
Good and Faithful Servant, buckle
  up, and get ready for the ride

All my love,
Daddy

What will the older version of you thank you for?

Dear Girls,

Lately, I've been looking at older people differently. Not with pity. Not even with reverence. But with a question.

What would they do differently if they could go back? Would they say "I love you" more quickly? Stop pretending to like things they don't? Spend less time on their phones and more time on the floor, playing with their kids?

In the quiet that follows, I realize I'm not thinking about them. I'm thinking about myself. I'm imagining myself at that age. And I'm asking myself those questions now, while I still have time to answer them with my life.

This isn't about fearing death. It's about fearing that I might miss it—the miracle of being alive—because I was too distracted, too numb, too performative.

I sat in a waiting room outside my therapist's office not long ago. Nothing dramatic. Just a tune-up for the soul. A girl beside me, maybe ten or twelve, sat next to her grandfather. They were talking about chili. About watching movies when they got home. About a school debate. It was small talk, but it wasn't small at all. It was love wearing everyday clothes. Then the grandfather stood up, walked into a therapist's office, and disappeared.

In that silence, I started asking questions I hope you'll ask one day not out of fear, but out of intention. What do older people think about when no one is watching? Do they feel proud? Do they wake with joy? Do they carry regrets they've never spoken aloud?

Regret is quite like that. It waits until the world has finally hushed. It waits until you're still enough to hear what you've avoided.

Another dad walked in the waiting room with his daughter, maybe six or seven. They talked about Kermit the Frog. She asked why he was wearing a suit. He teased, "Want a cup of coffee so you can wake up?" She didn't get the joke. He didn't mind. And I thought: We're all walking time machines. Every ordinary day becomes a memory or a miss. And our presence in these small moments shapes the person we'll become.

Girls, let me say this clearly: I didn't turn off my phone because I hated technology. I turned it off because I didn't want to wake up at eighty-six and feel like a stranger in my own story. I didn't want to scroll through your childhood. I wanted to live it. Even the hard parts. Especially the hard parts.

Please understand that I am not against cell phones by any means; I am merely against burdening regret—that may or may not surface for many years. I don't want to teach you how to be impressive. I want to instill in you the value of living without regret. It's about being present and making the most of every moment. Which means I have to risk it first. Risk being mis-understood. Risk not being liked.

I'm willing to show up, even when I don't have all the answers. Because I know you're watching, and I want you to see a man who is present, even in uncertainty. Because you're watching me. And one day, you'll either remember a man who was half-there, half-glowing in screenlight, or a man who was fully present. A little foolish, maybe. But free. And that's the man I strive to be for you. Awake.

Now, every day, I ask myself: What will the older version of me thank me for today? Sometimes, it's writing. Sometimes, it's saying no. Sometimes, it's putting down the grill tongs and running through the sprinkler with you, fully clothed, laughing like a lunatic. It's not perfect. But it's real.

If I get it right, maybe one day I'll look in the mirror, wrinkles and all, and whisper to myself, "We didn't waste it."

All my love,
Daddy

What if you still believed in yourself?

(DAY 331)

Dear Girls,

When I was younger, probably about your age, I believed in everything. The Tooth Fairy. Santa Claus. The Boogeyman. That if you cracked your knuckles, you'd get arthritis. That swallowing gum meant it stayed in your stomach forever. That a four-leaf clover could change your luck. That swimming right after lunch could be fatal.

Most importantly, I believed in myself. I believed I could do anything. Climb anything. Become anything. I believed in magic. In possibility. In wonder.

But as I got older, I started crossing things off the list, one by one. I started to doubt the things I once believed in. I started to doubt myself. I stopped believing in monsters. Stopped believing in tooth fairies. Stopped believing in the impossible.

And somewhere along the way, I almost stopped believing in myself, too.

During this year I turned off my phone, I started to feel it—that temptation to cross off the last thing. The most important thing. The belief that I could still do hard things.

Early on in the year, I was scared. I questioned everything. I wondered if I was being selfish. If I'd lose speaking gigs. If I'd lose connection. If I'd lose you. There were days when I felt so alone, I wasn't sure if I could finish. Days when the silence felt too sharp. Days when the doubt was louder than God's whisper.

But every time I wanted to quit, I thought about that little boy, the one who still believed. And I realized I didn't need to become someone new. I needed to remember who I was before the world told me to forget, and that journey of self-discovery was the most rewarding one. That belief, your belief in yourself, isn't childish. It's sacred. And I want you to protect it like your life depends on it. Because it does.

This year taught me that most people won't understand when you make a brave decision. And that's okay. In the beginning, they'll say it's unrealistic. Then, if you keep going, they'll say it's unlikely. But if you don't quit, eventually they'll say, "It was never in question." But it *was* in question. And that's what made it special. That's what made it real.

Girls, people will criticize you. They'll misunderstand you. They'll ask why you're doing what you're doing. They'll tell you it doesn't make sense—not because of cell phones, but because you dared to step outside the script. They'll criticize you for choosing rest when the world worships hustle. For telling the truth when silence would be easier. For staying tender in a culture that rewards hardness. For protecting your wonder when cynicism is the cheaper currency. They'll call you naïve for trusting God more than your résumé. They'll call you reckless for prioritizing presence over productivity.

But hear me: Every criticism is proof that you've chosen a different compass. And that's the only way to live a life that is yours, not theirs.

I want you to grow. I want you to chase wonder. I want you to remember that faith isn't loud. It's still. That God doesn't shout. He whispers. And He never stopped talking. We just stopped listening.

This year taught me that questions open doors. That silence holds answers.

I used to think I needed more time. But what I really needed was more clarity. More alignment. More truth. More childlike belief in the right things.

Here's what I came to believe: Presence is the greatest gift I can give you. Who I become will matter more than what I do. Legacy matters more than attention. Joy is still possible, even when life feels hard. Remember, the greatest compliment someone can give you is: "You've changed."

I hope you'll take a risk that no one else understands someday. And I hope you'll keep going because you still believe in yourself. I did this to show you it's possible. Not to be perfect.

Not to be productive. But to be awake. To be available. To be undoubtedly you.

If you ever feel lost, if the world tells you it's too late, or too much, or too different, ask yourself one question: What if I still believed in myself?

I think the answer will lead you home.

All my love,
Daddy

What if the hardest part is the finish line?

(DAY 336)

Dear Girls,

I used to think this journey would be like a marathon, a predictable path with clear milestones. At the start, you're surrounded by people. There's excitement. Endorphins. Hope. Then you hit the middle miles—quiet, gray, lonely. You can't see the end yet. It's just you and your breath. Just you and the road. One foot. Then the next. And usually, by the final stretch, the finish line gives you strength. Your pace picks up. The crowd returns. You feel lighter, even if you're hurting. Because the end is in sight.

That's what I thought this year would be like. It would be easy in the beginning. The hardest part would be the middle. That the final stretch would carry me home like a tailwind.

I was wrong. The hardest part wasn't the middle. It was the end. Not because I wanted my phone back. But because the silence had changed me and I was terrified no one else would understand who I was now. I'd spent a year listening. Slowing. Paying attention. But suddenly, all I felt was pressure. To write the book. To make it matter. To somehow justify what I'd just done.

And then came the questions. Why did I do this? Was it worth it? What if this whole thing fails—publicly, emotionally, spiritually?

And I carried that fear. That weight. That noise. Until it broke me. It happened in the car. You were both in the backseat. We weren't in a hurry. There wasn't a crisis. You were just being yourselves—curious, loud, and silly in the way kids should be. But something in me was already too full. Of frustration. Of fear. Exhaustion. Pressure. And it had nowhere to go.

At first, I asked you to stop. Then my voice got increasingly louder. I was no longer asking, but demanding. I turned the radio up as loud as it would go, not because I didn't want to hear you, but because I couldn't stand to listen to myself anymore. I tried to drown out your voices and my own. The voice that said, *You're in over your head. You've made a mistake. This whole thing was a selfish stunt, and now you've broken something that matters more than silence ever could.*

And then I screamed. Not a quick "Enough!" Not a snapped "Stop it." I screamed at the top of my lungs. For at least ten whole seconds. Ten seconds of rage, helplessness, and shame exploded out of me like a dam that finally broke.

You froze. Your little bodies stopped mid-motion. You looked at me with wide, startled eyes. And in that split second, when our eyes met, I saw something that undid me. I saw fear. Real fear. The kind that asked a question you were too young to speak aloud: Am I safe with him?

That broke me, girls. Not just because I'd yelled. But because I knew, deep in my bones, that I have one job as your father: to keep you safe. Not just with seatbelts or curfews. But with my presence. My energy. My tone. My love. In that moment, I hadn't kept you safe. I'd startled you. Shaken you. And the shame of that settled in like a storm cloud over my chest.

The silence that followed was much louder than anything that came before it. I pulled the car over and started sobbing. That was the lowest day I've ever had as a father. Not because I lost control. But because I felt like I had lost myself. You didn't understand why I was crying. You started crying, too. Because kids don't just respond to volume. They respond to energy. And mine was overflowing with fear.

I wasn't mad at you. I was terrified. Of being misunderstood. Of being judged. Of losing your trust. Of finishing this journey and still not being the man I wanted to be.

I need you to know this: That moment didn't define our relationship. But it did define a turning point in me. Because I knew I had to repair. I had to return. To you. To myself. To God. And I will spend the rest of my life making sure you know not that your dad was perfect, but that he fought like hell to become someone worthy of your love.

If you ever find yourselves at the edge of your capacity, if the tears come before the apology, if you break in front of the people you love most, I want you to remember this: You're not disqualified from grace. You're not broken beyond repair. You're not a bad parent. You're human. And what you do next is what will define you.

I held you both that night. I promised: Daddy's going to do better. Not just try harder. But dig deeper. Because that's what love does. It doesn't run from the failure. It roots itself in it. Love says that even when I fail you, I'll come back for you. Even when I shake the house apart, I'll rebuild it with softer hands.

That means showing you what safety looks like, even after the storm. Because the job hasn't changed. My job is to keep you safe. If this book, this year, this entire story boils down to one truth, maybe it's this: Becoming the father I want to be means facing the parts of me I wish you'd never seen. And every moment has a purpose to shape us. Even my lowest moment.

All my love,
Daddy

What are you really chasing?

Dear Girls,

It wasn't strange that I was being asked to speak. It was strange because of *where* I was being asked to speak. I had received an email from one of the executive pastors at our church, Mark. He had heard about my decision to live a year without a phone, a significant part of my personal journey, and wanted to meet me.

We grabbed coffee, and then he followed up a few weeks later to ask if I'd be willing to meet with our senior pastor, CJ. I wasn't looking to enter the spotlight, but CJ and Mark asked if I'd be willing to share my journey because it might speak to someone going through something similar. The series Mark and CJ had in mind was during March. With my background in officiating, they felt it aligned perfectly with my journey.

They wanted me to talk about basketball, officiating, faith, and this year without a phone. It was supposed to be an "interview," a structured discussion about my experiences, but it became something else, a profound moment of self-realization and transformation. A mirror. A marker. A moment when I realized how much had already changed.

Fast-forward to my interview with Kurt, another one of the executive pastors. He opened with a simple question: "How did you get into officiating?" I went back to sixth grade. To a kid with a temper who received too many technicals. I remembered the refs who took the time to talk to me. They didn't just make calls; they made contact. I didn't always agree with them, but I respected them. I told myself: One day, I want to be one of those refs.

And I became one. Not just in a middle school gym, but eventually in front of 15,000 fans. And hundreds of thousands more watching at home. I spent nearly two decades officiating men's college basketball. Most of that time was at the Division I level. And I wasn't involved only in college basketball, but also in USA Olympic training camps. I worked with legends: Coach K, Kobe, LeBron, Durant, and Anthony Davis when he was still "the kid."

Kurt asked me, "What's the best game you ever officiated?" People always expect me to name a buzzer-beater or a championship. But the answer is always the same: "The first practice with the 2012 USA Men's Olympic Team." Because it wasn't just the level of talent. It was the culture: a culture of humility, respect, and a relentless pursuit of excellence. It was the way grown men at the peak of their craft still took correction, wanted to grow, and remembered they were part of something bigger than themselves.

Then, we got into the meat of the interview. The part I never publicly acknowledged. Officiating wasn't tied to my identity; it *was* my identity. I didn't separate what I did from who I was. I told myself it was my calling. But the truth is, I had it all upside down.

My mentor, John Adams, told me at nineteen: Faith first. Then family. Then career. Then officiating. This order, John advised, is a guiding principle that can bring reassurance and direction in your life. But my reality was the reverse. Officiating was first, second, and third. If there was any time left for God, my family, or anything else, they had to fight for scraps. I was successful.

That's when I walked away from officiating. In my prime. No scandal. No injury. I couldn't name it then, but that chapter of my story was ready to be wrapped up. After years of being away from officiating, I realized that it was my training camp for life. It taught me how to lead. How to stay calm in chaos. How to make decisions under pressure. How to handle criticism. How to speak with clarity. How to stand still while the world moved fast. All so I could face what was coming. All so I could listen when God asked me to lay down the whistle.

And when my heart physically felt like it was giving out, when I found myself in a hospital bed, wondering if the double doors in front of me were the gates of heaven, God said: *Not yet. I'm not done with you. Buckle up for the ride.* And somewhere between the whistle and the Word, I realized: This isn't about my name in lights. It's about being faithful in the dark. If you're faithful with little, God says, He can trust you with more.

So, I'll keep showing up. Whistle or not. Phone or not. Platform or not.

Are you wondering if God can still use you after success, burn-out, misalignment, or walking away?

Yes. A thousand times, yes.

All my love,
Daddy

What's the rush?

Dear Girls,

There's a moment I look forward to every night. It's simple. Quiet. You probably won't remember it in complete sentences, but I hope your heart never forgets it. It starts after the stories are read and the prayers are whispered. After your stuffed animals are tucked under your arms and the lights are off. I pull the blanket up under your chins, kiss your foreheads, and leave your room.

Then I hear it. "Daddy...one more kiss."

I pretend not to hear you. I inch toward the door like I'm too far gone. But right before I step out, I turn. I run back toward your bed like I've just remembered the most crucial thing in the world. Because I have.

I plant another kiss on each of your cheeks and whisper something silly, something sweet. And as soon as I walk away again, you ask again. Or I do. We do it five, six, sometimes seven times. It's our little ritual now, a special moment we share every night, a testament to our love and bond. Our way of saying: I love you too much to leave yet; you are the most important part of my life.

But you don't know that this started as a lesson for me.

A few weeks into my year without a phone, I caught myself rushing through bedtime. Hurrying the hugs. Speeding through the stories. Whispering prayers with one foot already out the door. And I had to stop and ask myself: Why am I so hurried to leave the people I love the most?

Emails? They could wait. The dishes? They'd still be there. Even my writing, my work, my dreams? They were never more important than this. And yet, I was moving like they were.

One night, I sat on the edge of your bed long after you had fallen asleep. I stared at the ceiling and asked myself what I was really chasing when I rushed. Because it wasn't just about being busy. It was about being needed. About feeling important.

About convincing myself that I mattered somewhere out there.

But you know what? That kind of importance never held a candle to my presence beside your bed. You made me slow down, and in doing so, you taught me the true meaning of cherishing moments and the importance of being present. You made me remember what sacred actually feels like.

And girls, that's why I retired from officiating. Not because I stopped loving it. Not because I couldn't keep going. But because I didn't want to become someone who was celebrated in arenas and absent at home. I didn't want to be known as a great official if it meant being remembered as a distracted dad.

I traded the crowd's roar for the quiet of your laughter. I traded the court for the carpet next to your bed. And I'd make that trade every single time.

You see, love doesn't always show up in grand gestures. Sometimes, it shows up in staying. In saying yes when the world says, "That's enough." In turning around one more time for a kiss.

So, here's the one thing I hope you carry away from this: Don't rush the moments you'll one day ache to relive. Stay in the room a little longer. Take the detour. Say, "One more," when everyone else is moving on.

Because joy doesn't live in the highlight reel. It lives in the rewind button. And love? Love lives in the pause.

All my love,
Daddy

Can gratitude change a red light?

DAY 345

Dear Girls,

It started as a stall tactic.

We were driving to school one morning. It was chaotic, and you were both a little restless. Then we hit a red light. Giuliana, you released a theatrical sigh and said, "Why are we always stopped at red lights? This is taking forever." (For the record, it had been about seven seconds.)

So I said, "Okay, new game. Every time we stop at a red light, we say something we're grateful for." There was a long pause in the back seat as if I'd just suggested we recite the Constitution.

Then, Giuliana, you said, "The trees and the air." And Natalia, without missing a beat, you shouted, "Cookies!"

We laughed. And just like that, we had a new, simple ritual that made us feel at ease and comfortable.

We don't do it at every red light, but more often than not, before I even say a word, I'll hear it from the back seat: "Daddy, let's play the grateful game!"

And girls, here's what I want you to know: Gratitude is a choice. It's a pause button. It's a way of saying, "Even though I don't have everything I want right now, I can still love what I do have."

The world will try to make you impatient. It will convince you that waiting is wasted time. That red lights are interruptions. Delays are setbacks. But the truth is, red lights are invitations. They invite us to pause, to reflect, and to appreciate the present moment. They're invitations to slow down. To look around.

Remember that not everything is urgent, and some things are still sacred. Some things, like family, love, and nature, are always worth our time and attention. You don't have to wait for the big things to be grateful. You can be thankful for cookies. For trees. For air. For each other.

Someday, when you're sitting at a red light, maybe with kids of your own, I hope you'll remember this silly little game. I hope you'll start a new version of it. I hope you'll pass it on. Because it was never really about stopping. It was about noticing.

And sometimes, the most spiritual thing you can do is sit still long enough to say thank you.

All my love,
Daddy

Will you remember this like I will?

(DAY 347)

Dear Girls,

I asked you both what some of your favorite things to do with Daddy were. You didn't need long to answer.

Here are the things that make you both light up with joy:

- Making smoothies
- Flipping pancakes
- Having dance parties in the living room
- Jumping in the bounce house
- Getting tickled with the claw
- Pretending you're the teacher and I'm your student
- Playing soccer in the backyard
- Swinging at the park
- Requesting "one more kiss"
- Running races
- Blowing out the candle in my office

- Typing on my computer as if you're "working"
- Splashing in puddles with your rain boots
- Racing up the stairs
- Watching movies in your chairs
- Asking me to do "Silly Man"
- Holding my hand as we go up the stairs
- Coloring on paper in the kitchen
- Putting stickers all over me
- Reading books before bed
- Dressing up as princesses

And here is my favorite thing to do with both of you: spending any amount of time doing whatever it is you want to do.

Girls, here's the thing I need you to know: One day, you'll grow up and forget half the stuff on that list. But I won't. I'll remember the sound of your rain boots splashing in puddles. I'll remember how serious you got when it was your turn to "work" on my laptop. I'll remember how you both begged for "just one more story," like you were starving for magic. I'll remember the stickers, the claw, the way your hands fit inside mine.

These were never distractions from life. They *were* the life.

If you ever wonder what mattered most to me, it wasn't the emails or the inbox. It wasn't the goals or the grind. It was this. You. Us. Doing whatever you wanted to do. Together.

And if someday, when you're grown, and you wonder if your childhood was indeed big enough, magical enough, safe enough...please know that *you* were the magic, and I was always there, paying attention.

All my love,
Daddy

What if shedding isn't the end but the beginning?

(**DAY 349**)

Dear Girls,

I heard a word the other day, and it wouldn't let me go once I heard it. *Ecdysis.* It's the process a snake goes through when it sheds its skin. Not once. Not twice. Over and over again—up to twelve times a year. Shedding is not a sign of brokenness or flaw, but a necessary part of growth.

That hit me in a way I couldn't ignore. I used to believe that transformation was a single, shining moment. A bolt of lightning. A grand reveal. A before and after, like a home remodel on HGTV. But real growth? It's more humble. It's lonelier. It's the quiet recognition that the life you once fit inside has grown too tight, and staying within it would mean death. It's outgrowing the job. The habits. The stories you tell yourself. The fear of failing. The need to be seen. Even the way you cradle your phone or hold onto old skins like an oxygen tank.

And here's the wild part: The shedding is not graceful. It's not a gentle slipping away. It can be awkward, uncomfortable, and, more often than not, emotional. You might even grieve the person you are leaving behind. But if you don't shed, you suffocate.

It made me wonder: How often do we, as humans, shed our skin? Not just in theory. Not in a social media post. But in truth. How often do we leave behind a version of ourselves we've outgrown? Most people never do. Most people grip yesterday like it's a winning lottery ticket. On the surface, I gave up my phone to prove something. Or so I thought. Subconsciously, I did it because my life had grown too small for the person I was becoming.

I needed space to grow. Space to hear the quieter voice underneath all the noise. Space to notice what I'd been numbing. Piece by piece, layer by layer, I let go. I let go of the need to be constantly reachable. Of the illusion that I was indispensable. Of the comfort of distraction. Of the curated identity I had been so busy performing. And now, here I am, at the end of this year, standing on the trembling edge of what's next.

In just a few weeks, I'll turn my phone back on. And I am scared. I'm scared not of the device, but of the undertow it might pull me back into. Scared of forgetting. Scared of slipping. Scared of reaching for old skins that no longer fit. Scared of what I'll lose. Scared of what I'll find.

For the past year, I've been in a cocoon of sorts. Not protected, exactly, but pulled away. And in that space, I've grown. Not neatly. Not always gracefully. Yes, I missed some things. I missed text messages. I missed updates. I missed the convenience of reaching into my pocket and connecting with friends and family at the hit of a button. I missed headlines, highlights, and a thousand digital breadcrumbs the world wanted me to follow.

Because this past year wasn't a pause; it was a death. And that death demands mourning. For the convenience I've lost. For the version of me who needed so badly to be needed. For the ease of drowning in the familiar.

But here's what I've learned in the silence: Presence doesn't happen by accident.

It's a choice. An hourly, sometimes breath-by-breath choice to stay awake.

It's easy to slip back into numbness. It's easy to tape the old skin back on. But a snake doesn't apologize for shedding. It doesn't try to hold on to what it has outgrown. It just moves forward, raw and radiant.

Girls, listen to me: If you ever feel like you're breaking, maybe, just maybe, you're in the process of shedding your old skin. Trust it if you ever feel the ache of outgrowing a life that once felt safe. Shedding is becoming. And becoming isn't something the world hands you; it's something you claim.

Don't wait for the world to understand before you shed. Don't wait for comfort to tell you it's time. Don't wait for permission to be new.

Most people grip yesterday like it's oxygen. They stay wrapped in skin that no longer fits because the unknown feels too dangerous. But not you.

When your moment comes, and it will, I pray you have the courage to step into your new skin, all braided together to feel the grief, gratitude, and terror. Because growth isn't a destination. It's a series of tiny deaths and brave beginnings. And maybe the bravest thing you'll ever do is let yourself be reborn.

All my love,
Daddy

What if we knew it was the last time?

(DAY 351)

Dear Girls,

Last week, you sat at that little white table in the kitchen. You know, the one: two feet tall, covered in old stickers and marker smudges, just big enough for two tiny plates of macaroni or a tea party with stuffed animals.

You looked up at me with the kind of joy that still takes my breath away and said:

"Do Silly Man!"

I played coy. Pretended to need convincing.

You both nodded furiously. "Yes! Silly Man! Silly Man!" So I ran. Socks on, sliding across the hardwood, arms up, cheeks puffed, spirit fingers flailing, tongue out, making that ridiculous sound I somehow invented for your delight. You collapsed into giggles.

Belly laughs that made me feel like the wealthiest man alive. And in the middle of all that laughter, something hit me.

One day, without realizing it, I'll do Silly Man for the very last time. You'll outgrow it. Your tastes will change. Your sense of humor will mature. One day, you'll both say, "Dad, that's embarrassing," I'll smile and pretend it doesn't sting.

But that day wasn't today. Today, you asked for it again. "One more time, Daddy!" I gave it to you. Not as a performance. As a prayer.

A few months ago, I heard a concept called The Last Time. It's the idea that every ordinary thing we do—every mundane, repeatable moment—one day will happen for the last time. It's a reminder to cherish these moments, as we won't always know when it's the last time. There will be a last diaper change. A last bedtime story. A last walk to the bus stop. A last shout of "Daddy!" when you hear the garage door open.

Most of the time, we won't know it's the last. That's what breaks my heart.

That's what brings me back to life. Because when I remember that the last time is coming, I start treating this time like the gift it really is. Not just with you, but with all of life.

One day, I'll drink my last cup of coffee. One day, I'll lace up my running shoes for the last time. One day, I'll sit at this desk for the last time and write you a letter. I don't want to miss it. Any of it.

So, I'm learning to love the ordinary. To kneel down at the little table. To be silly. To be present. To be here. And I find the most extraordinary joy in these ordinary moments because you, my dear girls, make every moment memorable.

The truth is, I don't want to look back one day and wonder: What if I'd known it was the last time? I want to live in a way that makes every time feel like it could be.

All my love,
Daddy

What do I carry that belonged to her?

(**DAY 355**)

Dear Girls,

As the last week of my year without a phone began, I thought
the most challenging part was already behind me. I thought the
silence had finished its work on me. It had been a year of ups
and downs, high highs and low lows. I was battered but proud.
I could almost see the finish line.

I felt like there would be a version of me on the other side
that my family would be proud of. I had no idea another kind
of silence was waiting for me, and the race I was about to run
would be longer than any marathon.

Your grandma, my mom, had a doctor's appointment that week.
She had started experiencing short-term memory loss and was
struggling with basic arithmetic. We sought a second opinion,
hoping to rule out anything serious.

But the moment we sat down in the neurologist's office, I knew something was different. The room was cold—not just in temperature, but in feeling. Almost too quiet. Everything felt like it was waiting for something to happen. Three black chairs—stiff, standard, offering no comfort, just a place to sit while you wait—lined one wall. Across from them, there was the exam table with its thin sheet of crinkled paper, looking both clinical and vulnerable at the same time. The doctor's stool, a low, swiveling thing with wheels, felt out of place, almost casual in a space that demanded seriousness. The walls were neutral, like they were trying not to be remembered, and the air carried that faint, metallic scent of sanitized equipment and nervous energy. It was the kind of room that held silence like a bowl holds water, careful, heavy, and brimming with things unspoken.

Dad, Aunt Concetta, and I sat in those stiff chairs while Mom slouched on the exam table. We were there for almost three hours. It wasn't anything official. It wasn't a diagnosis. It was just a feeling. Something in the air had changed, and no one had named it yet. She forgot what day it was. Then she forgot what year. And when I reminded her, she looked at me like I was someone she used to know. Not a stranger. But not quite her son, either.

I didn't know grief could start before goodbye. I thought it would come all at once, like a wave. But in reality, it seeped in slowly, like watching her struggle to recall the name of someone she had just hugged. Little did I know she'd be gone less than four months later.

I'm not telling you this to make you sad. I'm telling you because this began a different kind of listening. I started paying attention to what she was leaving behind—not in boxes, but in me. And girls, let me tell you, I carry her. I carry her humor, the kind that loved to prank people at the grocery store just to get a laugh. I carry her stubbornness, the kind that wouldn't quit, even when it probably should have. I carry her faith, quiet, private, steady. The kind that didn't need to shout because it trusted. She wasn't loud about the things that mattered to her. She just lived them.

That's her when I pay for someone's coffee in line behind me. When I open a door and look someone in the eye, that's her. When I say, "I'm proud of you," for no reason, that's her, too. Sometimes, I catch myself saying something and think, "Wow. That sounded just like my mom." Sometimes, when I'm praying with you at night, I feel her presence in the room. I don't know how to explain it. It's not spooky. It's not strange. It's just her. Her warmth. Her stillness.

I've heard people say your parents live within you. For most of my life, it sounded like a nice idea. But now I know it's not just that. It's real. She's in my actions. She's in my way of noticing. She's in the way I love you.

That's why I wanted to write this. Because one day, if you notice your voice shaking a little when you speak up for someone...if you can't walk past a stranger in need without doing something about it...if you catch yourself smiling through tears while folding laundry...you might think of me. But really, it'll be her.

That's what legacy is. It's not what we leave behind. It's what we pass on.

If you ever ask: "Where did I get this fire in my belly?" "Where did I learn to hold a hand like it matters?" "Where did I get the courage to stay when things got hard?" You got it from me. And I got it from her.

All my love,
Daddy

What will I risk to tell the truth?

DAY 359

Dear Girls,

By the time you read this, you'll be older. Old enough to have your own memories. Old enough to understand that your dad is not a superhero, but just a man who decided to tell the truth. And maybe, just maybe, you'll be old enough to feel what I'm about to say.

This book, the one you're holding in your hands, is the most vulnerable thing I've ever created. I've shared things in these pages that I've never said out loud. There are moments here that broke me open. And I realize now, because I'm your dad, some people might use what I've shared to judge you.

Maybe they'll read this and whisper behind your back. Maybe they'll say, "Your dad was too much. Too emotional. Too raw." Maybe they'll laugh at the Silly Man stories or raise an eyebrow at the day I completely lost it in the car.

And I need you to know something: That was never my intention. But I'm not naïve to how the world works. People judge.
People mock. People shame. Some people use vulnerability as
a weapon. But you don't have to. You get to choose what you
want to find in the world. You get to decide what truly matters.

That's the deeper reason I'm writing you these letters. Because I
want to free you. To show you what it looks like to tell the truth,
even if it scares you. Even if it costs you something. And it will.
Even if someone doesn't like the version of you that finally feels
free. And yes, the values I hold may not be the same ones you
choose one day.

That's okay. But what I want you to remember is this: It's okay
to be vulnerable in the right spaces. It's okay to love with
your whole heart. It's okay to risk being misunderstood if the
alternative is living half of your truth. Telling the truth costs
something. It always does. But some things are worth more
than your comfort. Some things are worth more than your fear.

I chose to share my story because hiding it would have been a
much bigger loss. Because silence isn't neutral. Because pretending would have protected no one and robbed everything.
And if someone wants to judge that, so be it.

That's on them. Not on you. Not on me.

If you ever find yourself standing at the crossroads, fear pulling
you one way, freedom calling you another, I hope you remember: You are not here to live a curated life. You are here to live
a courageous one. One that you get to choose and don't need
to seek anyone else's approval for.

If someone ever tries to make you feel ashamed for being real, remember: They don't get to define your worth. They don't get to write your story. And they sure as hell don't get to keep you from living it.

My prayer is that these letters don't just tell you who your dad was, but that they also help you become more of who you already are.

All my love,
Daddy

What if I was angry at God?

DAY 363

Dear Girls,

There's something I've been dancing around this whole time.

I've written about silence. About doubt. About pain. About presence. About healing. About surrender. It felt like a slow ache in my chest that I didn't want to name. Because if I named it, I'd have to admit I was disappointed. I was mad and confused. No, I was angry.

Here I was, walking through this year turning off my cell phone, leaning into my faith, reading my Bible, and attending church every week—new routines that were happening as a result of this year without a phone. Trying to do what I thought God wanted from me.

And then your grandma got sick. And everything I thought was steady started shifting under my feet. I didn't say it out loud because I was trying to listen to God. But inside, I wasn't just screaming. I was spitting fire. I was daring God to answer me. "Why her?" "Why now?" "Why like this?"

I wasn't whispering polite prayers anymore. I was cussing into my pillow, pacing the hospital floors at 3:00 a.m., slamming my fists into the steering wheel and gritting my teeth, demanding answers: *This is what I get for being faithful?*

But the worst moment—the one I haven't told you about—was after your grandma had been on the ventilator for several days. I walked into that ICU room, and there she was. Tubes down her throat. Machines breathing for her. Her hands were tied down with soft restraints so she wouldn't accidentally pull the cords. The strongest woman I've ever known…silenced. Motionless. Speechless. Helpless.

I stood by her bed, and I couldn't feel God anywhere. All I felt was rage. And I didn't whisper it. I said it right there in that sterile room, not out loud, but inside, with a fury that shook every cell of my being: "You told me to obey. *This* is what I get?"

I wanted to scream. I wanted to rip the IVs out of the wall. I wanted to punch through the window. I wanted to believe in a God who wouldn't let this happen. And in that moment, I didn't. Because obedience didn't feel holy anymore. It felt cruel.

I know faith isn't a vending machine; you don't put in obedience and expect an easy life to fall out. Obedience doesn't come with an asterisk. It comes with assurance. But that assurance didn't feel comforting in that moment. It felt like silence. Somehow, in that silence, I realized I wasn't just mad. I was heartbroken.

When the people you love most start suffering? Something in you cracks. I wanted to believe He was still good. But I wasn't sure anymore. Not because I stopped believing in Him, but because I couldn't understand how pain and love could coexist.

And then...slowly, painfully, honestly...God asked me a question I couldn't shake: "Who is this really about, Me or you?" That question wrecked me.

Because it's easy to love God when your life looks like a highlight reel. It's easy to be grateful when the skies are clear, the test results are clean, and your family is healthy.

But can you still love Him when the world tilts? When the prayers go unanswered? When your mom forgets what day it is and doesn't remember your name? Can you still love God when the only thing left to hold is the ache?

I never once said, "This isn't fair." Not because I'm noble, but because I know better. If I say life isn't fair when it breaks me, I also have to say it wasn't fair when it blessed me.

It wasn't fair that I was born into this time, this country, this family. To the parents I had.

To the safety, love, and opportunity I was given.

It wasn't fair that I got the chance to turn off a phone and go searching for my soul while millions of people were just trying to survive.

So no, I won't say life's not fair. But I will say this: It's brutal sometimes. And beautiful. And sacred. And if I'm going to believe in a God who walks with me in the joy, I must let Him walk with me in the grief, too.

So yes, girls, I was angry. But now I realize what was underneath the anger: grief. And underneath the grief? There was love. And that love, the kind that can scream and still stay, that's the kind of faith I want to pass on to you.

Now, I want you to pause. Take a deep breath. Because what I'm about to tell you isn't just advice. It's the kind of truth that can hold your heart together when everything else feels like it's falling apart.

Here it is: God loves you. Not because you're good enough. Not because you try hard. Not because you pray the right way or say the right things. God loved you first. Before you even knew who He was, He picked you. And nothing you do can ever make Him stop.

You were made on purpose. You are not a mistake. You're not an "oops." You are God's brilliant, beautiful idea. And when God makes something, He makes it with meaning. That means you have a purpose, even when you feel small or unsure. God is closer than your next breath. Even when you can't see Him. Even when you can't feel Him. He's here. Right now. Listening. Loving. Holding you. He hears you every time you pray, whether it's a loud shout, a quiet whisper, or just a thought you can't even put into words. You matter to Him. All of you.

God can handle all your feelings, too. The big ones. The loud ones. The messy, tangled-up ones. Bring them all. He can take it. His words, the ones in the Bible, aren't old and dusty. They're a lifeline. A flashlight in the dark. A love letter with your name written all over it.

And when you mess up, and you will, God doesn't cross His arms and walk away. He forgives you. Every time you ask. No grudges. No "You should have known better." Just mercy. Fresh as morning sunlight.

Even when it feels like nothing is happening, God is working. He's weaving things together for good, even in the invisible places.

And guess what? God gave you special gifts to help heal and brighten this world right now. You don't have to wait until you're older. You don't have to be bigger. God is already ready. And the best news? God always wins. And if you're walking with Him, you win, too. Even when life feels heavy. Even when it's hard. He has already written the ending, and it's full of hope.

Sometimes, life will hurt. Sometimes, things will happen that you can't understand, and it's okay not to understand. It's not your fault. You didn't cause it.

And even when it feels unfair or messy, God's love for you doesn't flicker. You don't have to pretend you're okay if you're not. Your tears aren't a weakness. Your tears are a language God speaks fluently.

Even Jesus cried when someone He loved died. It's brave to feel. It's brave to grieve. It's brave to keep trusting God with a heart that's hurting.

And He promises: He heals every broken heart. It may not happen all at once. It might not be today or tomorrow. But your heart will smile again. Because we have a God who brings dead things, sad things, back to life. He's not done writing your story yet.

And I can promise you this: The ending is going to be beautiful.

All my love,
Daddy

Tomorrow, I'm turning my phone back on.

(DAY 365)

Dear Girls,

Tomorrow, I'm turning my phone back on.

I'll be doing a live interview at a local TV station to talk about what this year has been like. I'll even find out how many texts came in while I was away. I have no idea what that number will be. Maybe it'll be surprising. Maybe not. I just know I'll need to remember a charger. My phone hasn't been alive in a year.

When this year started, I thought I was doing something bold. A clever experiment. But instead, I walked straight into a funeral for a version of me I could no longer keep alive. For most of my adult life, I obeyed a god small enough to fit in my palm. It told me who to be, when to hustle, and how to curate my worth. And I listened. But what I realized is that in all the bedtime stories I often hurried through so that I could get back to my phone, I'd traded something important for something meaningless.

Girls, I hope what I've learned this year will be valuable to you. And although I wrote this book for you, I hope it will also be valuable to others. I hope people will finish the book and exhale. I hope they'll realize they're not broken. That the ache they've been carrying isn't weakness; it's wisdom. A call back to something more human, more sacred.

I hope that when they finish the book, they will look out and see their daughter laughing at the dinner table and stay there. I want them to hear their wife say something ordinary and actually listen. I hope they will feel their own heartbeat in a quiet room and not flinch from it. I want the book to end where real life begins. Not with more striving, but with stillness. Not with a to-do list, but with a homecoming. Because this isn't about becoming more efficient. It's about becoming free.

I don't want them to step into some grand vision of success-with-better-boundaries. I want them to step into their actual life.

We were never meant to be machines. Our worth isn't earned through exhaustion. We are allowed to stop running. We're allowed to be here.

Love is when your being becomes enough. Not the idea of love. Not the performance of it. But the kind that whispers, *Stay*, even when you want to disappear. The kind that looks like two little girls asking for one more bedtime story.

That is the call I almost missed.

All my love,
Daddy

Appendix

(**DID I MAKE YOU PROUD?**)

Dear Mom,

I'm writing this letter in the cemetery. Facing the mausoleum that says you're gone.

Your name is carved in stone, but I still keep hoping you'll answer when I ask:

Did I make you proud? It's such a quiet question, but now that you're not here to answer it, it echoes louder than ever.

I ask it over my morning coffee. I ask it when the girls say something funny you would have loved. I ask it in the silence after a long day. I ask it because you were the first person who ever believed in me. Before coaches. Before teachers. Before I ever even believed in myself. You believed in me so early, so completely, it felt like you whispered a secret into my soul, one I could carry into the world.

And now, I'm whispering it back into the silence, hoping you still hear me somehow.

It is often said that, among the many choices we make in life, the one thing we can't choose is our parents. While that's true, I won the lottery when it came to moms. And if I were given the choice, I would choose you again, every single time.

You were never just my mom, even though I'm an only child. You were everyone's mom. Aunt Boo to the world, but really, you were a second mother to anyone who needed one.

You turned every room into a living room. You made strangers feel like family before they even had a chance to earn it. You were joy in motion. You carried humor in your pocket like spare change, ready to toss it into any silence that needed light.

I carry your memories every day: Prank-calling Dad from across the room. Sneaking random items into strangers' grocery carts just to watch their faces. Giving someone a Get Well Soon card on their birthday, crossing it out and laughing until your sides hurt. You made the ordinary unforgettable.

And your heart? It didn't have borders. You gave away Christmas gifts to families you'd never met. Paid strangers' light bills. Served hot meals to people with empty plates and even emptier hope. When I asked why, you'd smile and say: "We have two choices in life: the easy choice and the right choice. The easy choice is always easy, but it's not always right. The right choice is always right, but it's not always easy."

In your honor, I'll continue to choose the right way over the easy way. Always. You didn't just talk about values. You lived them. Your life wasn't a speech. It was a sermon. And I'm still listening. You showed me that grief is a language no one teaches you how to speak. You showed me that life is fragile, that tomorrow is only an assumption, a concept, never a guarantee. You showed me how to squeeze every drop out of this life and love unapologetically, precisely how we all were meant to.

Nothing could have prepared me for the overwhelming void that your absence has left in my life. Grief isn't just sadness; it's all the things they don't tell you.

They don't tell you...

how the silence will be louder than a 757 at takeoff

and wrap you like a flannel blanket while sitting by a campfire

They don't tell you...

that your name will sound different

when it leaves my mouth

now that you're not here to answer it

They don't tell you...

how the world keeps spinning, even after yours stops

how the bills still come even though you don't feel like
getting out of bed

how strangers still laugh in public as if nothing happened

as if something sacred wasn't just snatched out of the sky

They don't tell you...

that every room becomes a museum

your picture a holy relic

your handwriting scripture

and every note from you, a prayer

They don't tell you...

that your scent clings to blankets like it's holding on for
both of us

They don't tell you...

that I'd memorize the sound of your voice

how it curled around "I love you" like it was trying to
shield me

from the storm you didn't see coming

They don't tell you...

to save random voicemails because one day

your name will stop popping up on my caller ID

They don't tell you...

that something so simple as a call on your birthday

is the only present you could ever ask for

They don't tell you...

that grief arrives like an uninvited guest

and refuses to leave

that it sleeps in your bed,

eats from your plate,

answers your phone,

and forgets to say hello

They don't tell you...

that I would miss your laugh

like I'm chasing an echo in a canyon,

or miss your loving touch

like I was still a kid,

and I've forgotten how to be held

They don't tell you...

that I'd miss your cooking,

your advice,

and your soft corrections

when I was too loud,

too proud,

and too much like you

They don't tell you...

that grief is a mirror

and when I looked into mine,

all I saw was your love—

love that was overflowing, untranslated, unfinished

I never fully appreciated

your presence

until I felt your absence

crack open the sky and pour down

in a language I'm still learning to speak

A language called I'm Missing You. A dialect called Why Now. And a silence called Forever. Because the one thing they don't tell you about grief is: The bigger the grief, the bigger the love.

I didn't know just how much I loved you until I saw how much of me broke when you left. And still, even through the ache, your love stays, warming my heart and guiding my steps. It's stitched into everything: the laughter of Giuliana and Natalia; the way they love without conditions; the way they laugh so hard their noses wrinkle, just like yours used to.

We often talked about the joys of parenting. You adored the girls. You adored being their Grandma. And I promise, Mom— they will always know who you were. We'll Be Like Boo. We'll carry your joy. We'll walk with your faith. We'll love like it's the only thing that matters.

You were there for my first breath. And when the moment came for your last, I wasn't there with you. I think about this a lot. Even though we shared private moments throughout your illness and on your final day, I couldn't bring myself to be in the room.

I'm sorry, Mom. But deep down, I know you wouldn't have held that against me. You were all grace. All kindness. All faith. People have thanked me for stepping up during your final months. But the truth is, you showed me how. Not with speeches. Not with declarations. But with presence. With quiet strength that held families together and made it look easy. You lived your values louder than words ever could. And even as your memory faded, your prayers never did.

Your faith wasn't a performance; it was your breath. You always encouraged me to chase my dreams, to think big, to believe.

I still have that book you gave me after I became a Division I referee. The one where you wrote: "You can achieve your dreams. Always think positive and big and it will be yours! Love, Mom."

Even though you never told me, I know exactly why you chose the song you did for our mother/son dance at my wedding. The song mentions six qualities: kind, sweet, gentleman, care, share, and be fair.

You didn't merely pick a song. You were leaving breadcrumbs to remind me when you were no longer here. And even when I didn't realize it, you were shaping the man I became.

I'll remember a lot from our time together here on earth. The most memorable: "You are the best thing that ever happened to me."

Mom, you were the best thing that ever happened to me. And even now, in the quiet moments, when the world gets too heavy, when the silence feels unbearable,

I whisper it again:

Did I make you proud? And in the marrow of my bones, I believe the answer is yes.

Rest easy, until we meet again.

Your loving son,
Tommy